ARCHERY

Steven Boga

STACKPOLE
BOOKS

To Robin Hood, who first got me interested in archery

Copyright © 1997 by Stackpole Books

Published by
STACKPOLE BOOKS
5067 Ritter Road
Mechanicsburg, PA 17055

Printed in the United States

10 9 8 7 6 5 4 3 2 1

First edition

Cover design and illustrations by Wendy A. Reynolds

Library of Congress Cataloging-in-Publication Data

Boga, Steve, 1947 –
    Archery/Steven Boga.
        p.   cm.—(Backyard games)
    ISBN 0-8117-2486-7 (pbk.)
    1. Archery. I. Title II. Series
GV1185.B54   1997   96-53457
799.3'2—dc21   CIP

CONTENTS

....

INTRODUCTION

· ·

Unmistakable sign you are at the Olympic
Games: A man walking through downtown
holding a handwritten sign reading:
"Need Two Tickets to Archery."
　　　　　　—Joan Ryan, columnist for the
　　　　　　　San Francisco Chronicle

I am a baby boomer and a member of the first television genera-
tion. And so, if you give me "archery" in a word-association test,
I say "Robin Hood." If you say "bow and arrow," I say "Indians."

Although as a kid I thought shooting flaming arrows from a
galloping pony looked like great fun, TV painted American Indians
in black hues, too evil to root for. Robin Hood, on the other hand,
could really set my heart aflutter, and it was he that I imitated
when I was in the backyard shooting arrows at cardboard boxes.

Robin Hood, the legendary hero of medieval England, was the
subject of nearly forty English and Scottish ballads and numerous
plays, tales, and films. Although constantly at odds with the sher-
iff of Nottingham, he was always loyal to the king, sometimes
identified as Edward IV (fifteenth century), sometimes as Richard
I (twelfth century).

Robin and his band—Little John, Maid Marian, Friar Tuck,
and the other men in tights—lived in Sherwood Forest in the English North Midlands, where they outwitted, robbed, and occa-
sionally killed the wealthy. The Robin Hood legend may have
sprung from the popular discontent that led to the Peasants'
Revolt of 1381.

Growing up watching the Robin Hood TV series, I cheered on
the Merry Men as I did the local football team. All I really knew,
or cared about, was that they robbed from the rich and gave to the
poor, and that Robin was the embodiment of excellence with a bow
and arrow. That man could shoot like Mickey Mantle could hit.
Taking almost no time to aim, he could hit an eye of a potato—or
the black heart of an enemy—from 200 yards. Even as a kid I

realized that I probably would never be that good at anything, but I knew that somehow if I could, it would be the greatest feeling in the world.

That must be how Justin Huish feels. U.S. archery got a big boost at the 1996 Summer Olympics in Atlanta when American archer Huish won the individual Olympic gold medal and then led the United States to victory in the men's team archery event. The twenty-one-year-old from Simi Valley, California, showed the guts of a tightrope walker when he nailed two 10s and a 9 on his last three arrows to help defeat South Korea 251–249. It was the first-ever team gold for U.S. male archers. Huish, a.k.a. "The California Kid," is a brash, gregarious lad, a rebel, and quite an image change for archery, which strikes outsiders as having about as much panache as shuffleboard.

Long after my days of shooting at cardboard boxes, I learned that archery lexicon includes the term *Robin Hood,* which occurs when an archer shoots an arrow and drives its tip deep into the end of another arrow already in the target. Archers display their Robin Hoods as golfers display their hole-in-one balls. I am not prepared to reveal how many of either of those trophies I have, but suffice it to say I haven't yet started work on a display case.

Of course, for some, archery's low-key nature is its very attraction. In my hometown of Berkeley, California, traditional archers meet regularly for shooting sessions that seem more like group therapy than sporting competitions. They decline to use sights, stabilizers, or torque-flight compensators, finding it more fun to "do that stuff in their heads." The group includes men, women, and children of all ages. According to Michael Lang, the driving force behind the group, "Archery touches something deep, something primal. Nine out of ten people who come once keep coming."

It's clear from the comments of these traditionalists that for them, archery is more meditation than sport, more therapy than competition. Says regular Dan Winheld, a printer, "It gives me a better attitude at work, where it's easy to get impatient." And psychologist Lucy Ferguson says, "When I'm arching, I'm working with myself and not at all self-conscious."

Lang, who is a history teacher, says that "sending one stick through space by arching another stick with a string gets your mind off your mind." He also believes that it helps teach discipline, concentration, restraint, patience, posture, breathing, anatomy, geometry, physics, vocabulary, history, anthropology, and the virtues of a democratic society. "In archery, children and parents stand together, facing a common direction," he says.

How truly refreshing.

• • • • •

My everlasting gratitude to the people everywhere who like to shoot and don't care if they kill anything.

Thanks also to the staff at the National Archery Association, who gave me help with a smile whenever I needed it.

HISTORY

No one knows exactly when the bow and arrow were invented. The discovery of vast quantities of neolithic arrowheads suggests they date back at least fifty thousand years, to the Solutrean period of the Late Stone Age. Some archaeologists estimate from cave drawings that the bow was in use at least one hundred thousand years ago.

The shortage of precise information about the origin of the bow and arrow doesn't in any way diminish the fact that they were one of mankind's greatest and most influential inventions, right up there with fire and the wheel. The bow allowed prehistoric humans to become proficient hunters, enabling them to kill prey from a distance. This improved the hunters' survival rate (hand-to-paw combat with a saber-toothed tiger was a dicey proposition) and added needed protein to their diet.

After humans moved out of caves and began to form empires, the bow and arrow continued to have a huge impact on their affairs. References to them appear in the earliest known writings and drawings all over the world. They are found in the Bible and in the preserved documents of all the ancients. Throughout most of their history, the Greeks and Romans used them as a military weapon. As their use continued to spread all over the world, the bow and arrow were also used for hunting and sport.

Empires rose and fell on the strength—or weakness—of the bow and arrow as a weapon. The ancient Egyptians first established the bow as a major weapon of war around 3500 B.C. They made arrowheads of flint and bronze and longbows almost as tall as themselves. Around 1800 B.C., the Assyrians designed a short composite bow of leather, horn, and wood with a recurved shape. More powerful than the Egyptians' longbow, it could be used on horseback, which gave the Assyrians an edge in battle.

The earliest Chinese known to history valued archery skills and held frequent contests. Early Mesopotamian and Hittite archers used a short recurved bow to shoot from light, fast chariots they developed around 1200 B.C. Persian archers who became skilled at shooting from horseback revolutionized warfare in the Middle East.

Middle Eastern superiority in warfare continued for centuries, largely on the strength of their better archery equipment and shooting technique. Although the Romans were renowned as mighty warriors, their archers used an inefficient draw to the chest and were outclassed by the third-century Parthians of Asia. The Mongols conquered much of Europe, and the Turks repelled the Crusaders, in large part because of their adroitness with bow and arrow.

In the Western Hemisphere, the American Indians were accomplished bowhunters. But their equipment was crude, and their success was mostly due to their uncanny ability to stalk within close range of an enemy or game. They contributed greatly to the development of field archery.

> To bolster the fighting skill of the peasantry, King Edward III of England (1327–77) banned all sports in his country except one—archery.

During the Middle Ages, in its simplest form, the bow was a single piece of springy wood, seasoned and shaped so that a string attached to its two ends caused it to bend in a regular curve, with the center of the bow stave farthest from the string. The dart or arrow was a straight shaft with two or more feathers at the rear end and a notch into which the string fit. A metal point was usually fitted to the front end of the shaft. Military arrows were sometimes barbed, other times rounded or fluted and waxed for penetrating armor.

Surprisingly, the crossbow—a bow mounted on a gun stock, with the bowstring drawn by a mechanical device—predates the longbow. Described by Pope Innocent II (1130–43) as "hateful to God and unfit for Christians," the crossbow was officially prohibited for use between Christian adversaries but permitted against the heathen Saracens. Although arrows fired with a crossbow

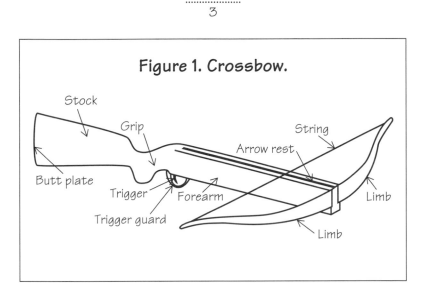

Figure 1. Crossbow.

could penetrate the inferior armor of the period, the crossbow became much less deadly once knights began to encase themselves in steel.

Most of the European bows before the Norman Conquest (1066) were of simple, single-material design, 3 to 4 feet in length. The longer Norse bows of the tenth and eleventh centuries, however, were among the best in Europe. Consequently, when William the Conquerer invaded England, his archers carried weapons far superior to the bows used by the forces of King Harold II. Historians give William's archers much of the credit for the pivotal victory at the Battle of Hastings. Their arrows fell behind the shields of the defenders, killing, among others, Harold himself.

Thereafter, the English abandoned their weaker and less accurate Saxon-style bow in favor of the longbow. The next five hundred years saw the most extensive use of the bow as a military weapon, with the true English longbow probably reaching maximum efficiency by the late twelfth or early thirteenth century. Ballads of the period, including the tales of Robin Hood, touted the skill of English longbowmen.

This simple but revolutionary weapon spread throughout England. Now a skilled archer could nock and fire six arrows per minute, striking a target 200 yards away with impressive accuracy. Arrows fired with a longbow, which had a greater force and range than the crossbow, were able to penetrate a 4-inch-thick oak plank or a suit of steel armor. According to one ballad, Robin Hood demonstrated the superiority of the longbow in an archery contest by shooting five arrows into the bull's-eye before his opponent could ready his crossbow for firing.

The longbow soon became the basic weapon of English armies, and a royal edict ordered all yeoman farmers to become proficient with it. The English bowmen of this period were the backbone of the most powerful infantry in the world and the first foot soldiers able to withstand and repulse the charge of the armored knights who had previously slaughtered them.

As archery became an integral part of man's lifestyle, the bow and arrow became a powerful symbol. Cupid and his bow symbolized love; the huntress Diana was pictured with a bow; the bow became a religious symbol to Zen Buddhists. Such a symbol of power is archery that it is represented on the Seal of the United States.

The greatest use of the longbow for military purposes was probably during the Hundred Years War 1337–1453, and the War of the Roses, 1455–85. The skill of the English archers was the deciding factor in such battles as Crécy, Poitiers, and Agincourt. At Crécy in 1346, the English army fielded about ten thousand archers against the French, although only slightly more than half were actually involved in the fighting, the others being in the king's reserve. Accounts from the time describe "arrow flights that darkened the sky," and a little math suggests that this was not hyperbole. Consider that each of the estimated six thousand fighting bowmen could fire about seven arrows per minute, with an effective range of about 250 yards. That's forty-two thousand arrows per minute, and this was bound to block out some sunlight. The arrows also pierced armor, brought down horses and riders, and threw the entire French advance into chaos. The slaughter of the French cavalry at Crécy was a memorable victory for the English infantry.

For the next two hundred years, the longbow and the power of the infantry were felt and respected wherever the English archers took a stand. Not until the sixteenth century, with the spread of firearms, was the longbow superseded as a weapon of war. It survived, however, as a hunting weapon and a sporting tool.

King Henry VIII promoted archery as a sport in England by ordering the establishment of an archery society, the Guild of St. George, in 1537. In 1545, Roger Ascham wrote *Toxophilus,* the first book to describe the proper way to shoot a bow and arrow. Archery societies cropped up throughout the 1600s, and their tournaments firmly established archery as a competitive sport. The Ancient Scorton Silver Arrow Contest, first held in 1673 in Yorkshire, England, endures today.

European settlers in North America brought their well-developed knowledge of bowmaking from their native countries, which spurred interest in target archery. The first archery club on this continent, the United Bowmen of Philadelphia, was founded in 1828.

In the aftermath of the Civil War, former Confederate soldiers were forbidden to carry firearms, prompting many to turn to archery. Two former soldiers, brothers Will and Maurice Thompson, learned to handle a bow and arrow with the help of Florida Indians. Maurice went on to write a book, *The Witchery of Archery,* which helped spread interest in archery across the country.

The National Archery Association was founded in 1879 and soon thereafter began holding national tournaments. Enthusiasm for bow-and-arrow hunting and for field archery—an event simulating hunting—prompted the establishment of the National Field Archery Association in 1939.

Archery made its debut as an official Olympic event at the 1900 Paris Olympics (the mythical founder of the ancient Olympics was Hercules, an archer). But after the 1920 Olympics in Belgium, archery was discontinued as an Olympic event and was not reinstated for fifty-two years. One factor inhibiting its international popularity in the early twentieth century was a lack of universal rules. The host nation typically held the type of competition most popular in that country. To broaden archery's appeal, a group of Polish archers assembled in the thirties to establish an international governing body. Their efforts led to the formation of the Federation Internationale de Tir à l'Arc (FITA), which established international rules and laid out the shooting rounds that were eventually adopted at the Olympic level. In 1972, archery was readopted as an Olympic sport.

The last thirty years have seen major technical advances in bow and arrow design, which have increased both shooting accuracy and enthusiasm for archery as a sport. A major turning point occurred in 1966, when H. W. Allen of Missouri invented the compound bow. It relied on eccentric (off-center axle) pulleys or cams, mounted in the tips of the bow limbs, to reduce the holding weight of the bow for a given draw weight. Although Olympic archery permits only the traditional recurve bow, there are plenty of compound bow competitions. The mechanical advantage offered by the compound bow has opened the door to a wave of new competitors who enjoy the challenge of combining personal skills with sophisticated equipment.

EQUIPMENT

··

A rchery is an individual sport requiring personalized equipment. Bows and arrows are sized for specific archers, and the notion that "one size fits all" is a misconception and a potentially serious safety violation.

Archery equipment is commonly referred to as *tackle*. The tackle required for target archery consists of a bow, matched arrows, a quiver, a shooting glove or finger tab, and an armguard. There also are other optional accessories.

THE BOW

For thousands of years after its invention, the bow was nothing more than a stick and a piece of vine used to launch a smaller twig. The stick gradually improved and the vine was replaced by string, but beyond that, changes were minor until the last fifty years, when technological advances converted the bow into a sophisticated tool. Today's high-tech models are made out of synthetic materials, no wood required.

Before you choose a bow, you must decide on your needs. The basic types of bows are the longbow, the recurve, and the compound. (The crossbow is beyond the scope of this book.)

Longbows. First, and for a long time, there was the longbow. Robin Hood is legendary for his use of a wooden longbow, but today most are made of fiberglass. The traditional English longbow is a D shape, but some old longbows are almost square, and others are close to round. Longbows range in length from about 5 feet, 6 inches to a little more than 6 feet.

Straight-limb fiberglass bows, though supplanted by recurve bows in serious archery, are still commonly used by schools and camps. They are relatively inexpensive, and the same bow will fit both right-handed and left-handed archers. A disadvantage,

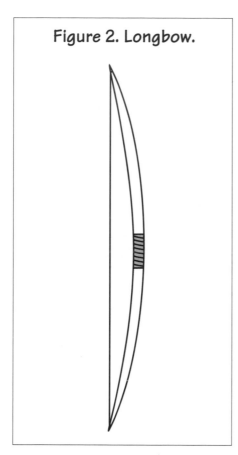

Figure 2. Longbow.

however, is that the straight-limb design doesn't provide much leverage, or cast, when the limbs are bent by pulling back the bowstring. Another is that the arrow sits either right or left of center on the bow, for which the archer must compensate when aiming. If the bow doesn't have an arrow shelf, the archer must support the arrow with the upper part of the bow hand.

Although there are traditionalists who still prefer the straight-limbed bow, none of them compete in the Olympics. A straight-limb is more difficult to master than a recurve bow, the type widely used in serious archery.

Recurve Bows. Most modern composite bows are constructed with a curve built into the tips, inclined toward the back of the bow. As the string is drawn, the curves in the limbs partially straighten, and their recovery to a C shape upon release adds to the speed of the arrow and thus to what is known as the bow's performance. Adding further to its performance is that the string's effective length is shortened on release as it comes to rest on the curve of the bow tip.

The ideal beginner's bow is a composite (wood and fiberglass lamination) recurve bow. Even inexpensive models are similar in design and shooting characteristics to the bows the experts use—the kind you will work up to if you stay with archery.

To maximize the leverage provided by the limbs, the bow must be fitted to your size and strength. Bows range in length from about 48 to 70 inches. Typically, shorter bows are used for hunting, longer ones for targets. They vary in draw weight (the pounds of force required to draw a bow a certain distance, usually 28 inches) from near zero (training bows) to more than 100 pounds. Most commercial bows fall between 20 and 70 pounds. The average draw weight for male tournament archers is about 50 pounds; for females, about 34 pounds. Field archery and long-distance target shooting usually call for a draw weight around 40 to 50 pounds. The practical minimum for hunting bows is about 40 pounds.

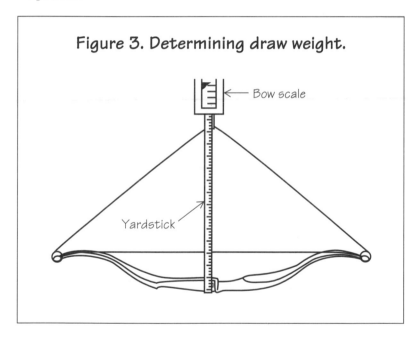

Figure 3. Determining draw weight.

Adult archers of average strength usually begin with a bow 20 to 25 pounds in weight; stronger archers may prefer 25- to 30-pound bows; young archers may need to start on bows as light as 10 pounds.

Former Olympic gold medalist John C. Williams offers this rule of thumb for selecting the draw weight of target archery bows:

Boys and girls ages 8 to 10:	10 to 15 pounds
Boys and girls ages 11 to 15:	15 to 25 pounds
Girls age 16 through adult:	20 to 35 pounds
Boys age 16 through adult:	30 pounds and up

Because draw weights are based on 28 inches of draw, you will have to adjust the figures if your draw length deviates from that. For each additional inch of draw length above 28 inches, add 2 to 2 ½ pounds of draw weight; for each inch below 28 inches, subtract 2 to 2 ½ pounds. Thus, if your draw length is 30 inches, you will actually be drawing 4 to 5 additional pounds.

Most archery manufacturers belong to the Archery Manufacturers Organization, but even those that don't have adopted AMO standards. Consequently, you can look on the bottom of the lower limb on the face of most bows and read the number of pounds of energy needed to draw that bow to 28 inches. For example, you may see 35# @ 28", meaning the draw weight for that bow is 35 pounds, assuming a 28-inch draw length.

To measure your draw length, stand about 25 feet from a target with a light-poundage bow and a long arrow. Holding the bow in the bow arm, extend it toward the target and draw back on the bowstring with the middle three fingers, bringing it back to the chin. Then ease the string back. Rehearse this several more times, making sure the bow arm is fully extended.

Now nock an arrow and lay it on the arrow rest. Draw the string back and have someone mark the arrow directly above the arrow rest. The distance from the nock slit to that mark is the draw length.

Your draw length as a beginner is likely to be shorter than it will be after a few weeks of shooting. With experience, you will learn to extend completely. If you decide to buy new equipment after your first archery lessons, remeasure your draw length.

Proper bow length is also important. It too is determined by your draw length.

Figure 4. Detail of grip and arrow shelf.

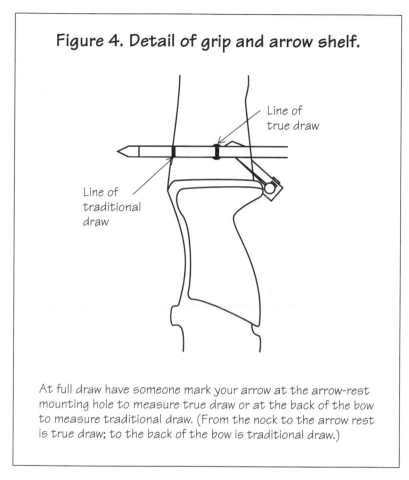

Line of
true draw

Line of
traditional
draw

At full draw have someone mark your arrow at the arrow-rest mounting hole to measure true draw or at the back of the bow to measure traditional draw. (From the nock to the arrow rest is true draw; to the back of the bow is traditional draw.)

Draw Length	Bow Length
Less than 24 inches	60 to 64 inches
25 to 26 inches	65 to 66 inches
27 to 28 inches	67 to 68 inches
29 inches or more	69 to 70 inches

Target bows for women and children are usually 62 to 66 inches long; for men, 66 to 70 inches long. Hunting bows are usually 52 to 62 inches long, as longer bows are unwieldy in the forest.

Be realistic when choosing a bow. Muscle strength is critical in determining proper draw weight, and archers tend to pick bows having more than they can handle. Too often the decision is made after one full draw, but the bow for you is the one you can hold comfortably for at least five seconds and shoot accurately over and over. Even though you may be able to draw and hold a certain draw weight, go to a lighter weight if you can't shoot it with some accuracy. You would be wise to start with a light bow that permits hours of practice with good form. You can change to a heavier bow as your skills improve.

In FITA competition, the unbraced bow complete with permitted accessories must fit through a hole having a 12.2-centimeter inside diameter, plus or minus. 5 centimeter.

State-of-the-art Olympic bow limbs are generally constructed of man-made materials, such as fiberglass, carbon, and synthetic foam. Bow handles are made of aluminum alloys and machined for strength. Some bow handles are made of a magnesium and aluminum mixture, which is heated to a liquid and poured into a mold. Once cooled, it is cleaned and painted.

Compound Bows. Compound bows have an eccentric (off-center) pulley or cam mounted on each limb tip. The pulleys are mounted so that the energy required to draw is greatest at mid-draw and smallest at full draw, when the archer is holding to aim. When the string is released, the energy applied to the arrow is increased. For example, an archer with a 50-pound compound bow of 50 percent reduction actually holds only 25 pounds of resistance at full draw, yet 50 pounds of thrust are imparted to the arrow.

Compound bows are typically made of layers of wood laminations and plastic with fiberglass reinforcement. Some manufacturers laminate four or five layers of fiberglass together to make high-strength limbs. These materials store and release energy with great efficiency.

Figure 5. Compound bow.

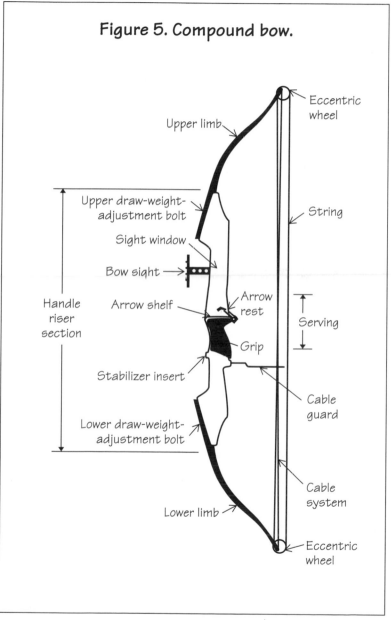

Like recurve bows, compound bows must be fitted to the archer's draw length and draw weight. Since the holding weight of a compound bow (the force at full draw) is a fraction of its peak weight, you can select a compound bow with a higher draw weight than your recurve bow. Of course, you will still need the strength necessary to pull through the peak weight.

Since the compound bow was first made available to archers in the late sixties, it has found many converts. Although it is allowed in some competitions, FITA regulations still require that the bowstring be attached directly between the two tips of the bow. Thus, the modern compound bow is not allowed in international meets.

ARROWS

> "No matter where I am, when a box of cedar arrow shafts is opened, I am once again twelve years old."
> —Larry Wise

The main parts of an arrow are the nock, cresting, fletching, shaft, and point. The nock is the small, molded plastic tip that fits over the string. There are several different types, the most popular being the snap-on, which snaps onto the string.

Cresting is the pattern of colorful rings around the shaft that distinguishes one arrow from another.

Fletching refers to the plastic vanes or natural feathers. These provide wind drag and cause the shaft to spin, which is essential for accuracy. Vanes are weatherproof and durable; feathers, by creating more drag, are more stable in flight.

Most arrow shafts are made of wood, fiberglass, aluminum, or carbon graphite.

Wooden Arrows. Wood, the material of choice since time immemorial, is still the choice of traditionalists and many beginners. Only in the last fifty years have arrows been made with materials that can outperform wood.

A quality wooden arrow shaft is flexible, strong, and durable. Wooden shafts are generally the least expensive, an important consideration for beginners. Good wooden arrows are tough enough to

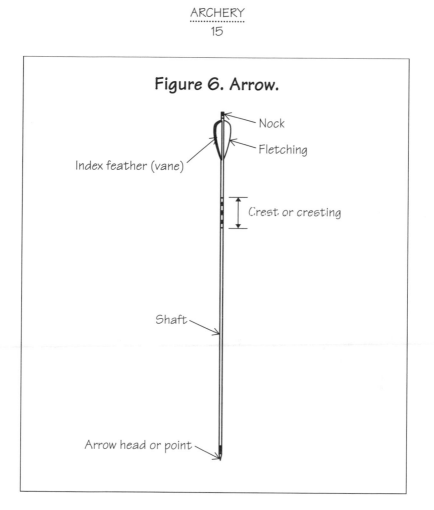

Figure 6. Arrow.

Nock

Fletching

Index feather (vane)

Crest or cresting

Shaft

Arrow head or point

withstand the punishment of many shots and capable of being straightened. The surface needs to be smooth, allowing it to pass the arrow rest cleanly. The diameter and density of all the arrows in your quiver should be the same to ensure consistent flight.

Although you can craft a wooden arrow out of almost any wood but eucalyptus, commercial arrows are almost always made of cedar, which is ideal for shaping, sizing, and hardening. Cedar has a straight grain that allows the arrow to bend as it passes the sight window of the bow, and then return to straight.

Shafts are usually sorted by spine value and marked with the draw weight range appropriate for that shaft. One spine value

The approximate arrow length for beginners can be determined by adding at least 3¾ inches to one's draw length. This provides a large safety margin. Intermediates, who presumably have developed a more consistent form, can use arrows 2 to 3 inches shorter than that.

Proper arrow length can be measured more precisely in one of two ways:

1. Draw a light bow with a long arrow that has been marked off in 1-inch increments, and have someone check the length at the back of the arrow rest. Beginners, who are unlikely to draw the same way every time, should draw several times to establish an average. When you have the arrows cut to proper length, make absolutely certain they are not too short. They can be slightly too long with no loss of performance, but arrows that are too short are dangerous.

2. Place the nock of a long arrow against the middle of your chest, with your arms extended in front of you, palms together. The length of the arrow is right for you if its point extends at least ½ inch past your fingertips (see figure 7).

might be suitable for a 30- to 40-pound range of draw weight, another for a 40- to 50-pound draw weight. If you use a 40-pound bow, you could use either spine, but you should probably choose the heavier, as it will recover more quickly in flight and be less susceptible to archer error.

If you take care of wooden arrows, they will last for years. Archer Larry Wise says he still has some of the first arrows he made thirty years ago. Store them in a dry place, as dampness can warp them. Check them often for splinters and cracks. Small splinters can sometimes be repaired with glue and sandpaper, but cracked arrows should be discarded.

When your arrow feathers get wet or ragged, you can return them to normal shape by placing them over the steam of a kettle

Figure 7.

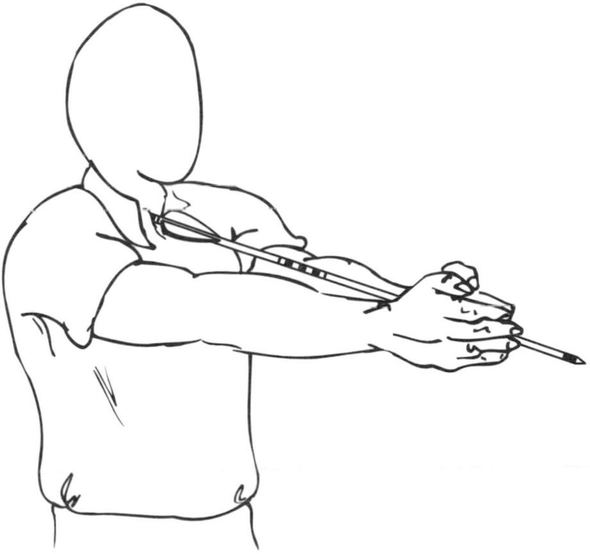

for a few seconds. If the feathers become too badly damaged, you can peel them from the shaft and refletch.

Fiberglass Arrows. Fiberglass arrows are the heaviest and therefore fly with a greater arching trajectory. They are expensive but resist warping.

Aluminum Arrows. Aluminum arrows have been available since the early forties, when James D. Easton developed the first trademarked aluminum shaft. Since then, aluminum arrows have been responsible for countless archery records.

There are about thirty different sizes of aluminum arrows available. The key variables are shaft diameter and thickness of the tubing wall. The size is printed as a four-digit number on the shaft near the nock end of the arrow. The first two digits indicate the outside diameter in sixty-fourths of an inch, and the second two digits indicate the wall thickness of the tubing in thousandths of an inch. Thus, a shaft size of 2315 tells you the diameter of the shaft is $^{23}/_{64}$ of an inch and the wall is $^{15}/_{1000}$ of an inch thick.

Arrow manufacturers have selection charts that enable you to match arrow size to your draw weight. Such a chart will help you determine the shaft sizes that will work best with your bow. Find three suggested sizes and test them all at your local archery shop.

Aluminum arrows should be checked frequently for kinks and bends. Bent aluminum arrows can be straightened with a mechanical straightener that has a gauge able to detect deviations to the nearest thousandth of an inch. Kinks usually cannot be straightened.

You can use soap and water, or even stronger cleaning agents, to clean dirty aluminum arrows. For grimy plastic vanes, use soap and water or denatured alcohol. If small tears or holes develop in plastic vanes, they should still perform properly. You can trim torn pieces with scissors and not affect the flight of the arrow. If most of a vane is missing, however, you should replace it.

> **T**oday's tournament arrows are made of either aluminum or carbon graphite. Aluminum arrows are more uniform in weight and shape; graphite arrows fly faster.

Carbon Arrows. Carbon, the newest shaft on the market, was developed in the late 1980s from resin-soaked carbon fibers. Carbon arrows have very small-diameter shafts that are stiffer than aluminum and lighter in weight.

Carbon arrows come in about ten different sizes and vary in diameter to match the most common draw weights and draw lengths of today's bows. With a diameter significantly smaller than an aluminum shaft, a carbon arrow is strong, stiff, lightweight, and swift. These high-tech arrows cost much more than aluminum arrows, but many top tournament archers believe it is a price worth paying.

ACCESSORIES

Armguard. The armguard, worn over the inside of the bow arm, is usually made of leather or plastic, though the Tower of London Armory displays one made of tortoise shell with silver fittings. A guard not only protects the arm from the sometimes severe slap of the bowstring, it also keeps long sleeves snug and free of the string.

Target archers favor shorter armguards that cover only the forearm from the back of the wrist to just short of the elbow. Hunters tend to favor longer guards that extend well above the elbow.

Shooting Gloves. You will eventually have to decide whether to draw the bowstring with your fingers or with a release aid. If you choose to use your fingers, as you must if you are vying for the Olympics, you may want to protect them with a shooting glove or a finger tab. Some hardy archers prefer to risk sore fingers for what they feel is a better touch.

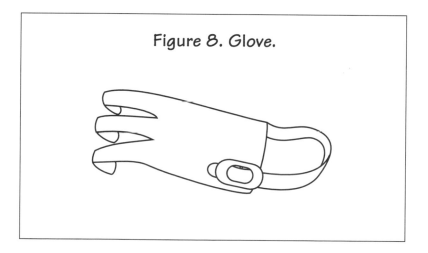

Figure 8. Glove.

Shooting gloves are made of leather and should fit snugly. Some hunters use a regular leather glove, but you need to cover only the two end joints of the three middle fingers, so a full glove is not necessary and may be counterproductive. Only the two end sections of the fingers should grip the bowstring for maximum control.

Each of the finger covers of an archer's glove has a strap that runs the length of the finger and joins the others on the back of the hand, where a wrist strap is fastened. Good shooting gloves have an adjustable wrist strap and quality stitch work at the seams.

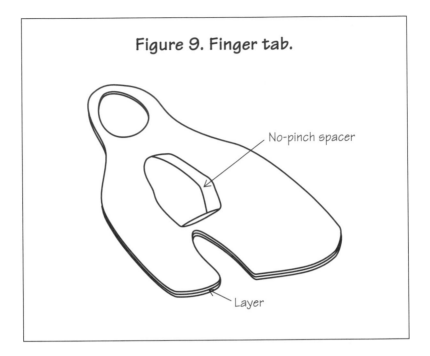

Figure 9. Finger tab.

No-pinch spacer

Layer

Finger Tabs. Popular among finger shooters is the finger tab, a flat piece of leather that fits over the three pulling fingers. Because the tab is one piece, it forces the fingers to work together when the string is drawn and released.

Like the shooting glove, the tab must protect only the first two joints of the fingers. The middle finger is inserted into a hole cut in the leather. Some tabs have a spacer to separate the middle and index fingers and prevent the archer from pinching the nock and throwing the arrow off-line.

The feel of the tab between your fingers is critical for a smooth, consistent release that disturbs the string as little as possible. Some archers prefer the feel of a tab with more than one layer of material. Although some choose two or three layers of leather, others prefer a layer of rubber or felt attached to the leather.

Wrist Sling. You want to maintain a loose grip on the bow so as to avoid applying torque and because duplicating a loose grip time after time is a lot easier than duplicating a tight grip. To prevent the bow from flying from your relaxed hand, you can tie a

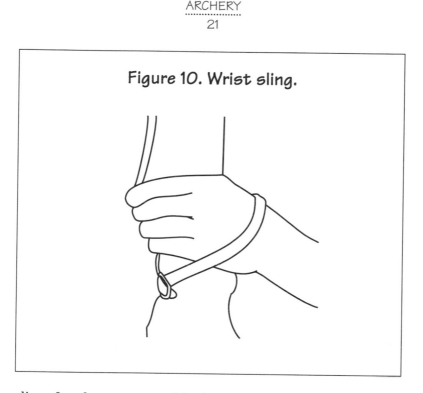

Figure 10. Wrist sling.

sling of cord or rope around both your wrist and the bow handle. Called a wrist sling, it can give you the confidence you need to relax your fingers and press only the palm of your hand into the handle grip.

Stabilizers. Stabilizers are small weights attached to the ends of metal rods that project from the back of the bow. Their added weight helps absorb vibration caused by movement of the hands and arms, making the bow feel sturdier. How much weight you add and where you add it ultimately depends on feel. Some archers like the weight close to the handle; others prefer it as much as 3 feet away. Weight may be added to the top, middle, or bottom of the handle, and some archers add weight to all three locations. Olympic archers have used as many as seven stabilizers on a bow.

Target shooters usually prefer longer stabilizer rods, which are better than short rods for balancing the bow and damping bow handle torque. Hunters generally use shorter stabilizers so that they won't get caught in brush.

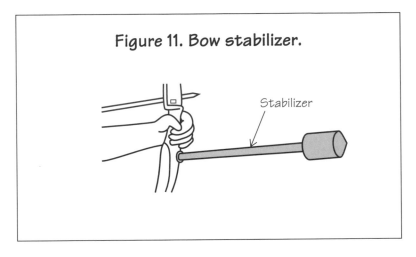

Figure 11. Bow stabilizer.

Stabilizer

ADDITIONAL ACCESSORIES

The following accessories are allowed in FITA competition:

Bow Sight. The bow sight is a sighting aid that, by rule, must be of simple construction and must not include any vertical rack and pinion or screw type of microadjustment. Lateral (windage) adjustment may be screw adjustable.

Draw Check Indicator. A draw check indicator is a device, such as a clicker, that tells the target archer that the arrow is fully drawn. It can be audible or visual but must indicate only draw length.

Dress Shield. A dress shield is a triangular piece of leather, plastic, or other material, fitted with straps, used to prevent the archer's clothing, from shoulder to chest, from catching on the bowstring when it is released.

Tassel. A tassel is a woolen cloth that hangs from the archer's belt or quiver and is used to wipe dirt from the shafts of arrows. Some clubs adopt a specific color for use by their members.

Mechanical Release Aid. About half of today's archers spare their fingers by using some type of release aid. Modern release aids rely on technology in the form of machined internal parts and molded exterior cases. The result is instant release of the bowstring when the archer operates a trigger mechanism.

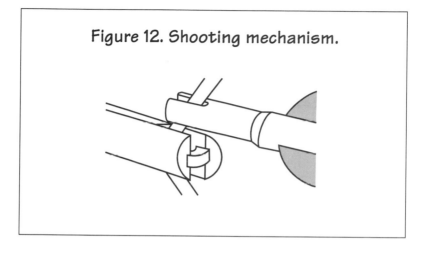

Figure 12. Shooting mechanism.

One type of release aid, preferred by most hunters, has a slot that fits around the bowstring and a metal gate that then closes around the string. Another type, the favorite of target shooters, has a small rope that fits around the bowstring and hooks into a slot and gate. Using either is much like using the trigger of a gun in that you must squeeze it slowly rather than setting it off quickly. As when shooting without a release aid, proper form requires good back-muscle tension throughout the aiming process.

Quiver. If you're a beginner and spent much of your childhood watching Robin Hood on television, you may imagine quivers, the containers that hold arrows, as made of deerskin and strapped to the archer's back. Actually, neither is true today. Although the back quiver enjoyed popularity for hundreds of years, it has been replaced by quivers that attach to the bow or the belt.

The bow quiver was designed about fifty years ago to make stalking game easier and quieter. Most bow quivers hold four to six arrows, neatly aligned, their points set in a foam-lined plastic cup to protect both the archer and the tips from damage. Most bow quivers are made from lightweight plastic and metal. Although mounting a quiver and arrows to the bow adds some weight, it's not enough to make the bow uncomfortable to hold for short periods. For tournaments, however, where competitors might make

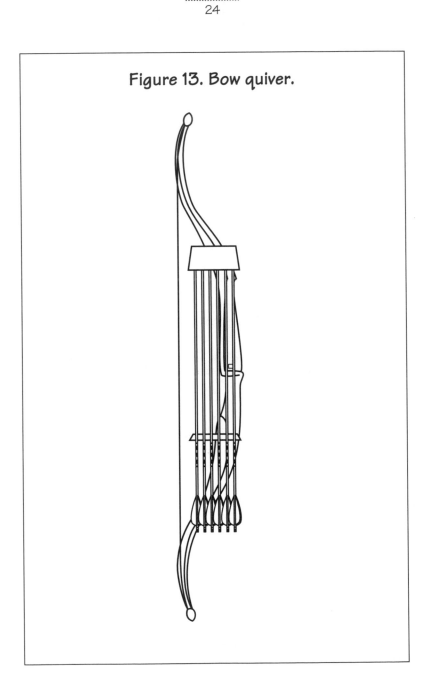

Figure 13. Bow quiver.

Figure 14. Belt quiver.

sixty or seventy shots, the extra weight would hamper effectiveness, and a belt quiver is more suitable.

Belt quivers, made from real or imitation leather or cloth, have one or more large compartments to hold up to three dozen arrows and several smaller pockets to hold small tools and spare parts.

Visual Aids. Field glasses, telescopes, or any other visual aid may be used to spot arrows only in the Olympic, Compound, and Barebow Divisions. They may not be used in general FITA competition.

Toolbox and Tools. You will eventually need tools and repair materials to make quick equipment repairs and adjustments. A well-stocked toolbox should include the following:

Tools

Allen wrench set
bow square
file
knife
needlenose pliers
nockset pliers
open-end wrenches
scissors
screwdrivers
small level

Repair Materials

dental floss
extra fletching
extra nocks
fletching cement
hot-melt glue
instant glue
monofilament serving
nylon serving thread

TECHNIQUE AND FORM

YOUR DOMINANT EYE

The first thing you have to do is to determine your dominant eye. Just as most people are either right-handed or left-handed, almost every person favors one eye over the other. To shoot a bow to your best potential, you should shoot on the side of your dominant eye, because the dominant eye automatically aligns any object projected in front of it.

It's easy and quick to find your dominant eye. With both eyes open, extend an arm and point your forefinger at some object across the room. Now close your left eye. If your finger is still centered on the object, your right eye is dominant; if the object is aligned with your finger when the right eye is closed, the left eye is dominant.

If you do most things right-handed but your left eye is dominant, you should learn to shoot a bow left-handed. By shooting on your dominant side, you can shoot with both eyes open, which lets in more light and allows for better depth perception. Besides, squinting or closing one eye shot after shot is hard work and leads to facial fatigue.

A small percentage of people do not have a dominant eye, and they may shoot from whichever side they choose.

THE STANCE

Archery form begins with the stance. Your goal is to be stable, comfortable, and relaxed. Only then will you perform consistently and efficiently.

There are three basic foot positions: open, even, and closed. To understand the differences between them, place an arrow on the

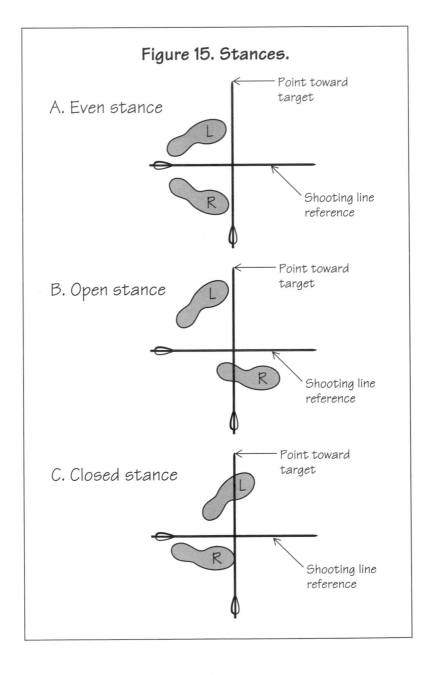

Figure 15. Stances.

A. Even stance

Point toward target

Shooting line reference

B. Open stance

Point toward target

Shooting line reference

C. Closed stance

Point toward target

Shooting line reference

ground parallel to the target face. That's your shooting line. Place another arrow across and perpendicular to the first arrow, pointing toward the target. Now straddle the shooting-line arrow, feet about shoulder width apart, toes splayed out slightly and touching the arrow pointed toward the target. This is the even stance, also called perpendicular or square.

To slide into the open stance, the one used by most archers, turn your face, chest, hips, and feet slightly toward the target. Slide the back foot forward until it rests on the arrow pointed toward the target. How far you open up to the target depends on how comfortable you feel and the results you get. Most archers find that the open stance creates a secure base, minimizes natural body sway and neck strain, reduces overdrawing, and provides maximum string clearance. Note, however, that if you open too much, you diminish the important role the back muscles play in the push-pull relationship during the draw.

To reach a closed stance, the least popular position, start from the even stance and slide the foot closest to the target forward, so that your foot is resting on the target line. The back foot pulls back ever so slightly from the target line, which orients your face and body farther from the target. The disadvantage of the closed stance for some archers is that it decreases string clearance and causes them to lean back and overdraw. The degree to which you close your stance should depend on how natural you feel and how well you do.

You may not find the perfect stance right away. As a beginner, be open to experimenting with foot position. When you find a position that seems to be working, stick with it through the slumps to give it a fair trial. The stance that feels most comfortable is probably right. Whichever one you choose, make a conscious effort to place your feet in the same position for every shot. This is the first step in developing consistency.

THE NOCK

Now it's time to nock an arrow. Holding the bow in the left hand, grasp the nock end of the arrow with the right hand and lay it across the arrow rest (left-handers should reverse these instructions). Now set it on the bowstring. The arrow should be nocked

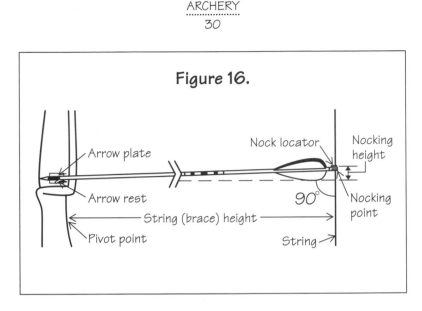

Figure 16.

between $\frac{1}{16}$ and $\frac{3}{16}$ inch above 90 degrees. To ensure nocking consistency, use a nockset locator, usually a small metal ring that is placed around the bowstring and pinched snugly with special pliers. The location of the nockset ring is critical for shooting accuracy. If it is even $\frac{1}{8}$ inch too low or too high, your arrows will fly with either a fishtailing or porpoising motion instead of straight toward the target. Make sure the nockset locator is movable so that you can adjust it as you go along.

Be sure the nock fits snugly on the bowstring so that the arrow doesn't fall off the string during the draw. Position the cock feather at a right angle to the bowstring, and the two hen feathers next to the string.

THE GRIP

The bow should fit in the V between thumb and index finger. Form a loose ring around the bow handle with thumb and finger, your hand conforming to its shape. The bow should press against the muscle pad beneath the thumb.

Most professional archers use a wrist sling to help secure the bow in the hand, then simply push against the bow handle with part of the palm. This allows them to relax the fingers and assures that no torque is applied to the bow during release.

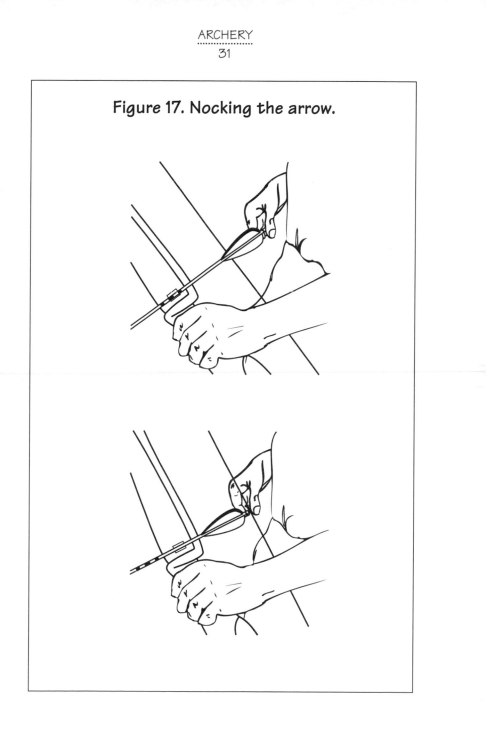

Figure 17. Nocking the arrow.

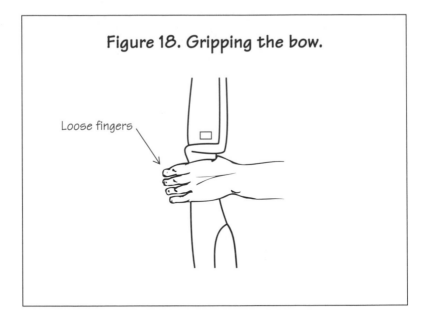

Figure 18. Gripping the bow.

Loose fingers

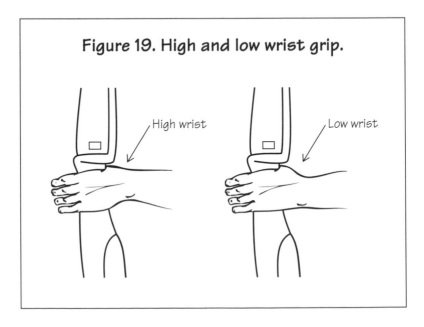

Figure 19. High and low wrist grip.

High wrist

Low wrist

You can position your palm either high or low on the grip. The high grip, with a stiff, straight wrist, places the pressure point nearest the arrow. The low grip demands a slightly bent wrist, with more of the base of the thumb riding against the bow grip. Give both methods a fair trial to determine which one suits you.

THE BOW ARM

You can extend your bow arm in one of two ways. Some believe it should be slightly bent at the elbow while aiming, but most prefer to have it locked straight. Beginners may find they are more consistent with a locked elbow, but as with most things, you will have to decide which style works best for you.

The shoulder of your bow arm must support the weight of the bow as you push it toward the target. It must also work in opposition to the muscles of the other arm that are pulling the bowstring. You can strengthen the shoulder through exercise, making it easier to maintain the down position. Lock your shoulder and push against a door frame for thirty seconds. Do twenty repetitions three times a day.

Whether or not your bow elbow is slightly bent, make sure you rotate the bottom of the elbow away from the string. This will give you better string clearance, keeping the string from stinging your bow arm on release. Until you consistently achieve proper shooting form, protect your forearm with an armguard.

Try to keep the bow shoulder locked in a down position. If you let it hunch up toward your chin during your draw and aim, you will lose stability and consistency.

THE STRING HAND

In preparation for the draw, place the three middle fingers of the string hand on the bowstring, the index finger above the arrow. The string should set deep in the crease of the first finger joints.

Figure 20. Holding the bowstring.

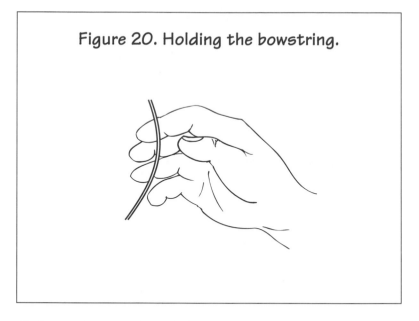

Curl your fingers around the string in the shape of a hook. Relax the wrist, maintaining tension in the fingers only.

POSTURE

A popular misconception is that archery demands strong arms and shoulders, but the critical muscles are actually in the back between the shoulders. These muscle groups work both together and in opposition to produce a clean release and follow-through. If they are taken out of the action, say by bending excessively, release and follow-through become ragged.

To make the most of those muscles, keep your back straight and upright. If you bend too far at the waist, you underutilize the back muscles and lose control. Likewise, your head should be upright and turned toward the target. We have muscles and tendons that connect the skull to the back, and if your head bends forward or to the side, those muscles and tendons will not work efficiently. Keep your head and back erect during the draw, and your back muscles can work directly against each other for a consistent release.

It will take weeks or months of conditioning to pre-pare your back muscles for the rigors of shooting dozens of arrows in a single outing. The principle of training specificity tells us that the best exercise is shooting arrows. But if you try to shoot seventy-five arrows on your first day, you will probably be sore enough to wonder why you didn't take up croquet instead. To assure that you stay with the program, start out slowly and build up to seventy-five or eighty arrows a day. Be patient but determined.

THE PREDRAW AIM

Set up about 10 yards from the target, with no bow sight. Before you even draw the bow, raise both your bow arm and draw arm to shoulder height. Keeping both eyes open, position the tip of the arrow about 18 inches below target center. Now shift your eyes back to the target center and focus there without moving the bow. This is called gap aiming.

Predraw gap aiming allows you to practice a consistent aiming technique prior to the stress of full draw. Doing it without a bow sight lets you concentrate on form.

Eventually, you will probably want to move back from the target and use a bow sight. A sight gives you a constant visual reference and allows you to direct your arrows to the same spot on the target shot after shot. If your arrows cluster outside the bull's-eye, you can use the sight to adjust future shots horizontally, vertically, or both. Trial and error will tell you how great an adjustment is needed.

THE DRAW

You must use your back muscles to push the bow arm toward the target and pull the other arm in the opposite direction. This push-pull motion must be in direct line with the arrow so as not to impart any torque to it.

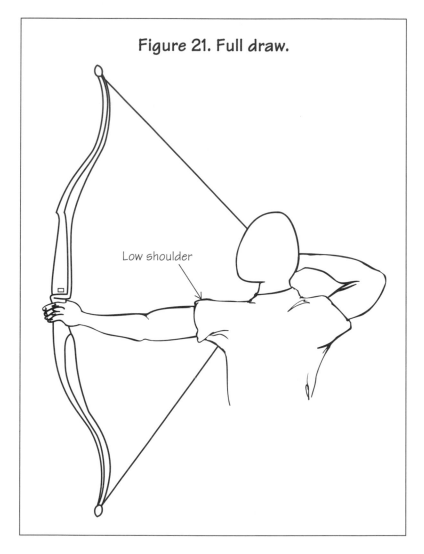

Figure 21. Full draw.

Low shoulder

Keep your head erect and draw the string back toward your face; don't move your face toward the string. Keep the drawing elbow above the drawing shoulder. If you continue to rely on the back muscles, you leave the arms relatively free of tension. Your shoulder blades should feel as though they're moving toward each other.

THE ANCHOR

As the drawing hand reaches your face, you must find your stopping point. It is essential that this anchor be secure enough that you always draw to the same position. A consistent anchor will increase your accuracy. There are two basic anchor options: high or low.

High Anchor. Some target archers prefer a higher side anchor point. It's comfortable, quickly established, and allows the archer to sight down the arrow shaft when shooting barebow. Disadvantages are that it may encourage overdrawing and creeping.

Rather than drawing the hand back under the chin, as you do with a low anchor, draw it straight back to the side of the face. Touch your forefinger (or a kisser button) to the corner of your mouth, and slide your thumb under your jaw. Keep the wrist straight, and relax the back of the hand.

Practice finding a consistent anchor spot using only your bow. Assume your stance, raise your bow, and draw to an under-chin anchor with your eyes closed. Feel for the proper position, hold for a slow count of three, then ease the bowstring back. Do ten successful under-chin anchors, then repeat for the side anchor.

Low Anchor. Most target archers prefer to bring the curled fingers back to a point just below the chin. This low, or under-the-chin, anchor prevents overdrawing, and its two-point contact on the chin and nose promotes consistency. The low position also allows you to shoot long distances with less sight movement, especially with lightweight bows.

When anchoring low, draw back close to the bow arm so that the string first contacts the nose and chin. The string, centered on the nose, bisects the chin. Touch the kisser button between the lips.

Although the low anchor is more popular, especially for beginners, you may find that the high anchor works better for you. Archers with large hands or short necks sometimes have trouble

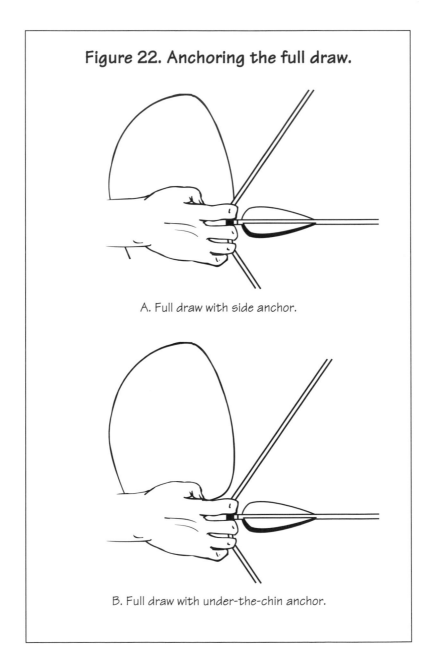

Figure 22. Anchoring the full draw.

A. Full draw with side anchor.

B. Full draw with under-the-chin anchor.

with the low anchor. As with many of the other variables in this chapter, experiment with different anchor positions to find the one that suits you. Any anchor position may feel awkward until you have conditioned your muscles through practice.

THE HOLD AND AIM

The aiming phase begins once you reach your anchor point. Whether you settle on a low or high anchor, maintain full draw by pulling steadily with the back and shoulder muscles. At this moment, your bow arm should be steady, your shoulder and back muscles locked. You are in the holding position and ready to aim.

For most archers, Robin Hood excepted, the aiming process takes about seven to fourteen seconds. Rather than alternating your vision between the target and your sight, relax your face and neck muscles, almost staring at the bull's-eye with a blank expression.

Take a deep breath and exhale as you nock the arrow, and repeat as you set your bow hand and string fingers. Take a final deep breath and exhale to a comfortable feeling during predraw. Maintain that comfortable feeling, without inhaling or exhaling, through the follow-through.

If something feels wrong—your concentration flags, the sight picture isn't right, your form feels off, or you've overheld—then let down and start over. Remember, your aim will only be as good as the form controlling it.

There are two basic aiming techniques: instinctive aiming and bow sight aiming.

Barebow or Instinctive Aiming. If you don't use an aiming device, such as a bow sight or point-of-aim marker, you may use a technique called instinctive aiming. The basic technique of the hunter and the barebow class of field shooting, it is essentially aiming by trial and error, relying on experience to improve accuracy.

Bow Sight Aiming. The bow sight is an attachment to the bow that places a marker or aiming aperture in the bow window. To aim, you must line up the aperture with the bull's-eye rather than looking at the relationship between the arrow and the bull's-eye.

Almost every target archer uses some kind of bow sight, from a simple pin taped to the back of the bow to a sophisticated sighting device. Sights are especially effective when shooting from fixed distances. Since bow sights are calibrated by distance, knowing how far you are from the target makes them very effective.

Most commercial bow sights have a sight pin that is fixed on the target. The pin is adjustable so that it can be set to predetermined distances. If you are shooting from 25 yards and the pin settings are in 10-yard increments, merely aim midway between the 20- and 30-yard pin settings.

Bow hunters often rely on bow sights too. Since they seldom know the exact distance to the target, the pins are used as reference points. Once a hunter can estimate the distance to his target, he can adjust his aim accordingly. Some hunters like to color code their pin sightings, making it easier to locate the correct sight pin when speed is of the essence.

Once you have made your pin selection, shoot a few arrows, noting where they hit relative to the bull's-eye. Then move the sight pin from the center to the cluster. If the arrows are low, for example, move the sight pin down. Once the sight position is determined and set, it should remain unchanged for that distance, assuming no change in form or weather.

Before you release, make sure the sight is locked on the bull's-eye, not just passing in front of it.

THE RELEASE AND FOLLOW-THROUGH

Finger shooters should release the string as the release hand is being pulled directly away from the target. As this occurs, maintaining intense back and shoulder tension allows you to relax your string fingers (rather than forcing the fingers open). All three fingers should come off the string at the same time.

After the release, the bow arm should drop slightly and the release hand should stay high as it moves directly away from the target. If the release hand does not pull directly away from the target, the fingers will hang on to the string too long, precluding a clean release. These motions should follow from proper push-pull tension and not be forced by the archer.

Shooters using a release aid rely on the same basic push-pull sequence. When the sight pin is aligned with the center of the

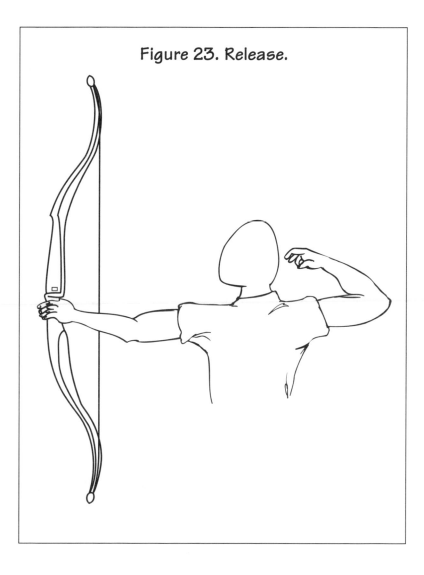

Figure 23. Release.

target, the archer begins the push-pull motion, simultaneously squeezing the trigger or rotating the handle of the release aid. If the push-pull is ragged, the release hand won't draw back directly from the target, adversely affecting the string—and your accuracy.

When the string is released, the back and shoulder muscles relax, causing the bow arm to drop slightly and the release hand to continue on its path behind the ear of the archer. Called the follow-through, it's the muscles' natural reaction to the buildup and release of tension. If the push-pull motion is executed properly, the follow-through should fall into place. Neglecting the follow-through can cause the bow arm to drop before the arrow has actually left the string or rest.

Even after release and relaxation of back and shoulder muscles, the head should stay erect, eyes on the target center. The shoulders should be moved down and back, not collapsed. The bow arm remains extended, with little movement. The fingers holding the bow remain relaxed. The string hand lies back along the side of the neck, fingers relaxed, free of tension.

Let the arrow enter your line of sight. Don't try to find the arrow as it leaves the bow, lest you pull your head, moving your shoulders and arms and throwing the arrow off-course before it clears the arrow rest.

Hold the follow-through until you hear the arrow hit the target. Concentrating on the bull's-eye will prevent flinching and peeking. It's critical that your form remain positive and consistent and not fall apart upon release.

FORM ANALYSIS

Go through the entire shooting sequence in front of a full-length mirror. Try different angles. Pay particular attention to your anchor point and follow-through. If you can, have someone video-tape you. Watch the video over and over, preferably with someone who has a critical eye. Look for flaws. A video camera is a wonderful teaching tool for aspiring archers. It will make it easier for you to develop a mental image of the proper shooting form.

Here's a checklist to help you analyze your form:

Stance

_____ Straddle shooting line.

_____ Align feet so that toes are on target line, or adjust slightly to open or closed stance.

_____ Stand with weight evenly distributed.

_____ Stand erect with shoulders back and level.

Hold bow forward and nock arrow the same way every time.

Draw and Aim

_____ Set and relax bow hand.

_____ Form hook with draw fingers, index finger above arrow.

_____ Keep draw hand wrist straight but relaxed.

_____ Turn head to look over front shoulder.

_____ Raise bow and rotate bow elbow down.

_____ Keep bow shoulder down.

_____ Draw string back by pulling back on elbow at shoulder level.

_____ Anchor under chin so that string touches nose and chin.

Release and Follow-Through

_____ Tighten back muscles and maintain full draw.

_____ Bring sight to target as you aim.

_____ Focus on center of target.

_____ Concentrate on maintaining tension in back muscles.

_____ Relax entire string hand and let string slide through fingers in a smooth, straight line.

_____ After release, keep bow in line with target and eyes on bull's-eye.

GETTING BETTER

....

You can detect and correct errors in archery by focusing on your technique and your results, both means and end. Review the preceding chapter and strive to create a mental picture of proper form. Constantly observe the details of your stance, draw, anchor, hold, release, and follow-through, staying alert to tension in specific areas of your body that suggests improper alignment.

As you fine-tune your form, your arrows should start to cluster in patterns. The location of this cluster relative to the bull's-eye can tell you a lot about both your strengths and weaknesses. Analyze your patterns periodically to correct errors before they become habits.

ARROW PATTERNS

In the beginning, before you have developed any consistency, you will probably see a scattered-arrow pattern—that is, random misses mixed in with occasional hits. This suggests a host of errors, the antidote for which is practice. As you eliminate beginner's mistakes and continue to navigate the various plateaus on the trail to perfection, you should find that your arrows tend to group left, right, up, or down. The cause of these misses could be equipment setup, or it could be a consistent flaw—or flaws—in your technique. Congratulations—you've come a long way since you were making mistakes inconsistently.

Shot locations can be described in terms of a clock face. Arrows hitting to the right of the bull's-eye are 3 o'clock errors, arrows hitting below center are 6 o'clock errors, and so on.

Correcting 12 o'clock Arrows

1. *Error:* You grip the bow too low on the handle.
   Correction: Move your hand up and check for consistent placement on every shot.
2. *Error:* The arrow is nocked too low.
   Correction: Relocate to proper nocking position and strive for the same position on every shot.
3. *Error:* You anchor with your mouth open.
   Correction: Keep your teeth together but not clenched.
4. *Error:* You anchor inconsistently.
   Correction: Use consistent anchor; use kisser button.
5. *Error:* You lean away from the target.
   Correction: Stand up straight and distribute weight evenly. Use back muscles to draw.
6. *Error:* Your bow arm is extended more than usual, which increases draw length and draw weight.
   Correction: Move draw elbow back.
7. *Error:* Your elbow points downward during the draw.
   Correction: Move draw elbow back to shoulder level.
8. *Error:* The heel of your hand pushes on the bow handle at release.
   Correction: Transfer pressure to the upper center of the hand; keep the bow hand relaxed throughout the shot.
9. *Error:* You inhale just before release.
   Correction: Exhale and hold before aim and release.
10. *Error:* Finger pressure on string is uneven.
    Correction: Form hook with all three fingers supplying equal pressure. Draw with back muscles, bring draw elbow back at shoulder level, release string by relaxing fingers.
11. *Error:* Your chin drops down to anchor.
    Correction: Keep your head up. Bring the string to your head rather than the opposite.
12. *Error:* You hold your head too far back.
    Correction: Place your chin on the draw hand and your nose on the string, and maintain head position throughout the shot.

13. *Error:* You fail to take into account a strong tailwind.
    Correction: Use your head. Wait out strong gusts. The more experience you have shooting in wind, the better able you will be to compensate for it.
14. *Error:* You aim too high.
    Correction: Shoot plenty of arrows and note your results. Make adjustments.

Correcting 3 o'clock Arrows

1. *Error:* Your bow tilts right.
   Correction: Before sighting, check the limbs for verticality, using peripheral vision or the level on your sight aperture.
2. *Error:* You grip the bow handle too far to the left.
   Correction: Position the bow hand so that the forearm takes the force of the bow resistance as the string is drawn.
3. *Error:* You look inside of the string (between string and bow), creating improper alignment.
   Correction: Before aiming, align the bowstring with the middle of the limbs and just to the right of the aperture. Using a peep sight, center the target in the sight.
4. *Error:* You employ an improper stance, addressing the target off-center.
   Correction: Adjust your stance so that an imaginary line through your toes intersects the bull's-eye.
5. *Error:* Your bow wrist breaks left on release.
   Correction: Relax the bow hand and wrist throughout the shot.
6. *Error:* Your bow arm moves to the right on release.
   Correction: Relax your bow hand throughout the shot and follow-through. Stay focused on the bull's-eye until the arrow lands.
7. *Error:* Your draw fingers tighten during hold, or your hand plucks the bowstring on release.
   Correction: Increase back tension while aiming. Keep the back of your draw hand flat, the draw hand relaxed, and release the string simply by relaxing the fingers.
8. *Error:* You lean forward.
   Correction: Stand up straight and distribute your weight evenly. Keep your feet, hips, and shoulders on the target line.

9.   *Error:* You anchor to the left of your normal position.
      Correction: Draw straight back to your anchor position, close to your bow arm.

10.   *Error:* Your head moves forward during draw and anchor.
      Correction: Stand up straight and keep your head up, weight evenly distributed; bring the string back to your head.

11.   *Error:* Your chest collapses, relaxing your back muscles.
      Correction: Increase back tension during the hold.

12.   *Error:* You fail to factor in a left-to-right wind.
      Correction: Use your head. Wait out strong gusts. The more experience you have shooting in wind, the better able you will be to compensate for it.

13.   *Error:* You peek to watch the arrow in flight.
      Correction: Stay focused on the bull's-eye until the arrow lands.

Correcting 6 o'clock Arrows

1.   *Error:* You grip the bow too high on the handle.
      Correction: Move your hand down and check for consistent placement on every shot.

2.   *Error:* The arrow is nocked too high.
      Correction: Relocate to proper nocking position and strive for the same position on every shot.

3.   *Error:* Your draw stops before reaching the anchor position.
      Correction: Bring the string all the way back until it touches chin and nose.

4.   *Error:* You anchor higher than usual.
      Correction: Use consistent anchor under the jawbone; use kisser button.

5.   *Error:* You grip the bow too tightly, developing tension in the hand.
      Correction: Increase back tension during the hold; relax the bow hand.

6.   *Error:* Your bow shoulder rides up during the draw.
      Correction: Extend bow arm toward bull's-eye; use back muscles to draw.

7.   *Error:* You lean forward or your head moves forward.
      Correction: Stand up straight and keep your head up, weight evenly distributed; bring the string back to your head.

8. *Error:* Your bow wrist is too high.
   Correction: Relax the bow hand; draw with your back muscles.
9. *Error:* Your bow arm bends or drops at release.
   Correction: Keep the bow arm extended toward the bull's-eye until the arrow lands.
10. *Error:* Your draw hand creeps forward prior to release.
    Correction: Hold steady, coming to a full anchor point before release; increase back tension; use clicker.
11. *Error:* You use a *dead release,* extending the fingers to let go of the string.
    Correction: Increase back tension during the hold; pull the draw hand back at release so that it recoils over the rear shoulder.
12. *Error:* You exhale on the release.
    Correction: Inhale and exhale before aiming.
13. *Error:* Your chest collapses, relaxing your back muscles.
    Correction: Increase back tension during the hold.
14. *Error:* The arrow hits your bow arm or clothing.
    Correction: Rotate your bow arm down before drawing; wear tight-fitting clothes or use a clothing shield; open stance slightly.
15. *Error:* You fail to factor in a headwind.
    Correction: Use your head. Wait out strong gusts. The more experience you have shooting in wind, the better able you will be to compensate for it.
16. *Error:* You aim below the gold.
    Correction: Do not release until the bow sight is aligned with the gold.

Correcting 9 o'clock Arrows

1. *Error:* Your bow tilts left.
   Correction: Before sighting, check the limbs for verticality, using peripheral vision or the level on your sight aperture.
2. *Error:* You grip the bow handle too far to the right.
   Correction: Position the bow hand so that the forearm takes the force of the bow resistance as the string is drawn.

3. *Error:* You grip the bow too tightly.
   Correction: Hold loosely, using a bow sling to provide security. If no sling is used, form a ring around the bow with the thumb and forefinger, keeping the rest of the fingers relaxed.

4. *Error:* Your eye lines up the bowstring too far right of bow sight.
   Correction: Before aiming, align the bowstring with the middle of the limbs and just to the right of the aperture. Using a peep sight, center the target in the sight.

5. *Error:* Your bow wrist breaks right on release.
   Correction: Relax the bow hand and wrist throughout the shot.

6. *Error:* Your bow arm moves left on release.
   Correction: Relax your bow hand throughout the shot and follow-through. Stay focused on the bull's-eye until the arrow lands.

7. *Error:* Your draw fingers tighten during hold or your hand plucks bowstring on release.
   Correction: Increase back tension while aiming. Keep the back of your draw hand flat, the draw hand relaxed, and release the string simply by relaxing the fingers.

8. *Error:* You squeeze the arrow nock with your draw fingers.
   Correction: Place fingers above and below the nock, and use your back muscles to move the bowstring.

9. *Error:* You nock the arrow with the index feather down.
   Correction: Place index feather toward you.

10. *Error:* You lean backward.
    Correction: Stand up straight and distribute your weight evenly. Keep your feet, hips, and shoulders on the target line.

11. *Error:* Your draw stops before reaching the anchor position.
    Correction: Bring the string all the way back until it touches chin and nose.

12. *Error:* You anchor to the right of your normal position.
    Correction: Draw straight back to your anchor position, close to your bow arm.

13. *Error:* Your head moves forward during draw and anchor.
    Correction: Stand up straight and keep your head up, weight evenly distributed; bring the string back to your head.

14. *Error:* Your chest collapses, relaxing your back muscles.
    Correction: Increase back tension during the hold.
15. *Error:* The arrow hits your bow arm or clothing.
    Correction: Rotate your bow arm down before drawing; wear tight-fitting clothes or use a clothing shield; open stance slightly.
16. *Error:* You fail to factor in a right-to-left wind.
    Correction: Use your head. Wait out strong gusts. The more experience you have shooting in wind, the better able you will be to compensate for it.
17. *Error:* You push or stiffen the bow arm on release.
    Correction: Relax and hold correct position throughout the release and follow-through.

PRACTICE

You've heard it for years: "If you want to improve, you have to practice." Indeed, it is the willingness to practice that separates masters from the middling, no matter what the pursuit. As sports philosopher George Leonard says, "The master of any game is generally a master of practice."

There's the old story of the Texans driving through New York on their way to a concert. They stop to ask directions.

"How do you get to Carnegie Hall?" they ask an old man.

"Practice . . . practice," he answers.

The master's journey begins as soon as you commit to learning a new skill, whether it's how to knit, cook, weld, or play dominoes. But sports provide an especially effective launching pad for the pursuit of excellence, because the results of training are clearly visible. In most sports, you can plot your progress, either with statistics or by comparing yourself with other players.

It's important to understand that the master's journey is not an inexorably upward slope. Instead, it consists of brief spurts of progress, each followed by a slight decline to a plateau usually somewhat higher than the plateau that preceded it. It looks like this.

Figure 24.

Clearly, then, you have to be prepared—and content—to spend a lot of time on plateaus; you have to push yourself to practice even when no progress is evident. Only with diligent practice will you imbed the shots in muscle memory, the behavioral autopilot that works subconsciously.

Even if you're bursting with talent, practice is essential; in fact, you may have to practice harder, because we tend to ease up when skills come easily. We're tempted, in George Leonard's words, "not to penetrate to the marrow of a practice." Rather than being frustrated with plateaus, learn to revel in them. If you can enjoy them as much as the upslopes, you are on the path to mastery.

According to George Leonard, author of *Mastery*, there are five keys to opening the doors to mastery:

1. **Instruction: Be open to first-rate teaching.**
2. **Practice: Think of the word as a noun, not just a verb, as something you are, not just something you do.**
3. **Surrender: Give in to your teacher and the demands of your discipline.**
4. **Intentionality: Muster all the mental energy and vision you can behind the pursuit.**
5. **The Edge: Push yourself beyond your ordinary limits.**

PHYSICAL FITNESS

You can be a couch potato and still shoot an arrow. But if you get even semi–serious about archery and want to improve, you should prepare your body by doing specific exercises. If you doubt that target archery is a physically demanding sport, consider this: The average draw weight of a man's bow is 50 pounds, and in an average tournament, the bow is lifted and drawn more than 312 times, for a total of 15,600 pounds, or 7.8 tons. Women pull about 5.3 tons with their 34-pound average bows. And this is while trying to maintain full concentration the whole time.

The accurate shooting of an arrow demands precise control of your physical movements. In target archery, you must reproduce, as identically as possible, for shot after shot, the individual movements in the shooting sequence. Having the strength necessary to accomplish this will greatly boost your coordination, confidence, and enjoyment of the sport.

Physical fitness has four components:

1. Cardiorespiratory endurance—the sustained ability of your heart and blood vessels to carry oxygen to your body's cells.
2. Muscular fitness—consists of both strength, the force a muscle produces in one effort, and endurance, the ability to perform repeated muscular contractions in quick succession.
3. Flexibility—the ability of your joints to move freely and without discomfort through their full range of motion.
4. Body composition—refers to how much of your weight is lean mass (muscle and bone) and how much is fat.

Fitness needs to be specific to the tasks you wish to perform. Judging fitness on the basis of bulging muscles or the ability to run a six-minute mile misses the point for archers. Although *aerobic* exercise (a continuous, rhythmic exercise during which the body's oxygen needs are still being met) boosts cardiorespiratory fitness and is important for general health, it is not as essential as muscular fitness for archery.

Although leg and hip muscles are important in archery, the muscles of the upper body are most critical. The flexors and extensors on the drawing-arm side of the body are needed to help hold a standing archer's body with proper alignment and rigidity. The same muscles on the bow-arm side of the body help balance this control, although they don't provide as much strength.

As you raise your bow and hold it in position, the deltoids raise the arm, with some help from the supraspinatus muscles. The pronator teres muscle rotates (pronates) your elbow out of the

Figure 25. Muscles used in bow draw and release.

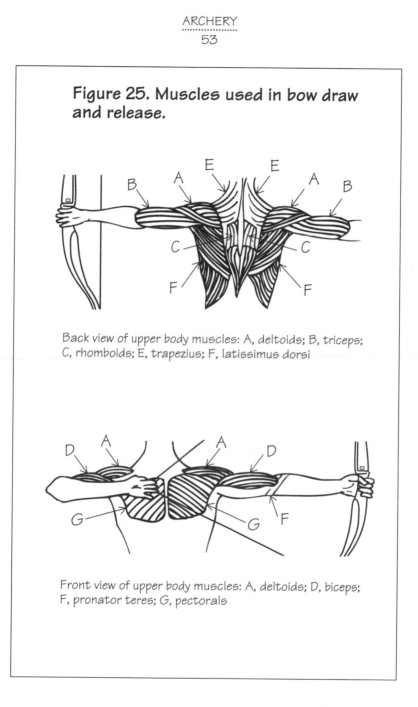

Back view of upper body muscles: A, deltoids; B, triceps; C, rhomboids; E, trapezius; F, latissimus dorsi

Front view of upper body muscles: A, deltoids; D, biceps; F, pronator teres; G, pectorals

string path. Flexor and tensor muscles on both sides of your bow forearm hold your wrist firmly in a static contraction to resist the pressure of the bow. Triceps keep the bow arm extended; biceps on the bow arm are relatively relaxed. The sternomastoid muscle on the drawing-arm side of your neck, the muscles on the bow-arm side of the upper spinal region, and some of the upper trapezius muscles all rotate the neck and help you hold a strong, relaxed head position.

When you draw, the drawing-arm muscles are in dynamic contraction. The biceps of the drawing arm contracts your arm into the proper angle. The rhomboids (probably the most important muscles in the draw-aim-release sequence) and middle trapezius muscles draw your shoulder blades together. The lower trapezius keeps your shoulder blades from hunching up. Minor pectoral and subclavian (under the collarbone) muscles hold the bow-arm shoulder down. Continued back tension is assisted mainly by the posterior deltoid, infraspinatus, and teres minor muscles, with some help from the latissimus dorsi. When releasing the string, the archer maintains back tension while relaxing the flexor muscles in the fingers.

EXERCISES

Studies show that the upper body suffers the most neglect. Even people who get enough cardiorespiratory exercise may not be able to do a single push-up. Women tend to be especially weak in the upper body, with weakness along the back of the upper arm a common problem. And men with firm biceps may have weak, shapeless muscles in the shoulders, chest, and back. Because they are so neglected, the muscles of the upper body often respond most noticeably to conditioning.

To develop the muscles necessary to control a bow, you must push them through an overload training program. Begin such a program well before the start of the archery season. Combine pushing exercises with pulling exercises to prevent imbalances that put weaker muscles in jeopardy.

Push-ups. Push-ups can quickly strengthen shoulders, arms, and chest. Using the weight of your body for resistance, this classic exercise overloads the front deltoids, pectorals, and triceps and requires little or no special equipment.

Figure 26. Push-ups.

A. Modified

B. Classic

C. Deltoid

The push-up is not an easy exercise. Many women cannot initially do one full push-up, and men who don't regularly exercise the upper body may also have trouble at first. If that's the case, start with the modified push-up until you can do twenty without pause, then move on to the classic push-up. If even the modified version is too strenuous, start by doing the exercise standing and leaning against a wall. Increase the angle and the number of repetitions until you can switch to the floor.

Do the modified push-up on your knees, with your ankles off the floor and crossed and your hands beneath your shoulders. Keep your torso straight and firm as you lower your chest to the floor and push back up. Avoid locking your elbows in the up position.

When doing the classic push-up, place the burden on the front of the shoulders by balancing your weight between your hands (placed under the shoulders) and your toes, which are flexed. Align your body so that it is straight. Keep it rigid as you lower your chest to the floor. Do not rest between push-ups or lock your elbows.

To work on your chest, position your hands a little wider, point your fingers straight ahead, and keep your elbows close to the body. To tone triceps, place your hands close together and point the fingers toward the center of the body, splaying out the elbows.

By raising up at the waist and bearing the weight of your torso on your shoulders, you make your body into a bridge, toning the deltoids and firming the trapezius. Keep your elbows slightly bent even when you are fully raised, and keep your body bent at the same angle as you slowly lower your head to the floor.

As you improve, you can do raised push-ups with your feet resting on a step or a stool. The higher you raise your feet, the more weight shifts onto your upper body, intensifying the effort. The ultimate upper-body builder is a handstand push-up done against a wall, but most archers will find the above versions sufficient.

Dips. Another effective exercise requiring limited equipment is the dip, which targets the rear deltoids, triceps, lower pectorals and trapezius, and latissimus—important muscles for an archer. Like the push-up, the dip uses body weight to overload muscles that don't ordinarily have to provide much body support.

Figure 27. Dips.

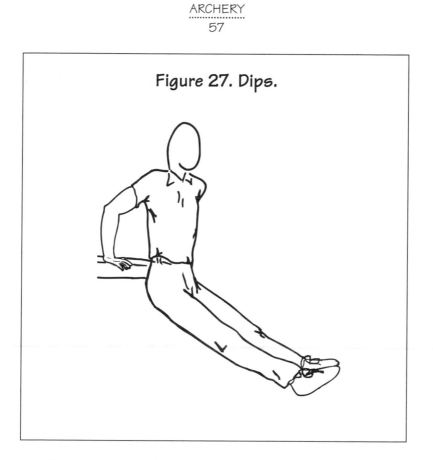

With a stool, weight bench, or sturdy, well-balanced chair behind you, lean back on your hands, balancing on your heels. Keep your shoulders down, the top of your chest up, and your back straight. Bend your arms and lower yourself without hunching your shoulders toward your ears. Straighten your arms to push yourself back up.

Dumbbell Bench Press. Using small weights lets you isolate muscles better than exercises that rely on body weight alone. Three- to 5-pound weights work well for most women, though many will prefer more weight for bench presses. Most men will do well with 7- to 10-pound dumbbells, though again many will want to increase the load for bench presses.

The bench press tones the shoulders and chest. Lying on your back, hold the weights just above chest level. Raise them straight up without locking your elbows, then slowly lower them.

Bench flies work the pectorals, the major muscles that shape the chest. With light weights in each hand, move your arms out to the sides, forming a cross. Keep your elbows slightly bent and your back flat on the bench. Raise the weights in a semicircular arc until they are side by side above your chin. As always, breathe evenly throughout the exercise.

To isolate the triceps, grab both ends of a single dumbbell and hold it several inches behind your head, with your forearms bent at a right angle. Raise the weight until it is high over your chest.

To exercise the latissimus dorsi, hold one end of a dumbbell in one hand and extend it as far beyond the top of your head as possible. Slowly raise the weight until it is over your chest, keeping the elbows unlocked.

Bent-Over Dumbbell Lifts. To do a bent-over lift, which firms the latissimus, trapezius, rhomboid, and biceps, bend your knees and lean forward at the hips. Keep your back straight and your buttocks high. Reach down, grab a dumbbell with each hand, and lift them straight up.

From this position, you can do bent-over double flies, which emphasize the latissimus. Let the weights hang easily below your shoulders, then slowly lift up and to the rear.

Doing single lifts will protect the lower back. Bend over with your knee and non-weight-bearing hand resting on a weight bench, and lift straight up.

Do single-arm flies for latissimus, triceps, and trapezius by supporting knee and hand on a bench. Start with the weight in the bent arm at the side of the chest, and extend your arm to the rear.

Standing Dumbbell Lifts. Upright lifts work the shoulders, biceps, and forearms. Spread your feet slightly farther apart than your shoulders. Lean forward a little to avoid arching your back. Hold a weight in each hand down at thigh level, then slowly lift them straight up the front of your torso as far as your collarbone.

To work the deltoids, do a standing lateral raise. Start with a relaxed posture, dumbbells parallel to each other in front of the groin. Slowly lift them out to the sides until your arms are parallel to the ground, keeping your elbows slightly bent.

Biceps and Triceps Dumbbell Curls. Curls focus on the biceps. While seated, spread your legs and lean forward, resting

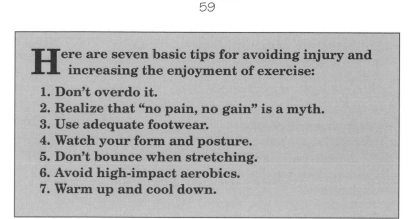

Here are seven basic tips for avoiding injury and increasing the enjoyment of exercise:

1. Don't overdo it.
2. Realize that "no pain, no gain" is a myth.
3. Use adequate footwear.
4. Watch your form and posture.
5. Don't bounce when stretching.
6. Avoid high-impact aerobics.
7. Warm up and cool down.

your empty hand on your thigh. Holding the weight in the other hand, curl it up and in, with your elbow pressed against the inner thigh. Continue the movement through a full range of motion.

Double curls work both arms simultaneously. Sit up straight, with your shoulders down and the weights held at your sides. Curl the weights up to your collarbone, being careful not to bend forward or arch your back.

To isolate your triceps, sit up straight and fold your arms over your head. Hold the end of the dumbbell in one hand, and use the other hand to steady the weight-bearing arm. Raise your arm above your head without locking your elbow.

Pull-ups. With a chin-up bar, you can use all your body weight for upper-body resistance. The chin-up quickly gives muscles an intense workout, but it requires so much strength that you might have to work up to it.

A bent-arm hang with your legs supported is the easiest way to work the chin-up bar. Place your feet or calves on a stable object to support part of your weight. Hold the bar with palms in, elbows bent. Hang in this position for thirty seconds or as long as you comfortably can. Rest for thirty seconds and then repeat. When you can do this easily, do pull-ups with your legs supported.

The next level of difficulty is the bent-arm hang with the legs unsupported. Grip the bar with the palms facing in and the elbows slightly bent. Lift your legs and hang for as long as you can, trying for gradual improvement. When you can hang for forty-five seconds, try a standard pull-up.

Despite good intentions, half the people who take up a new exercise program quit within six months. Here are six ways to boost your stick-to-itiveness:

1. Seek convenience.
2. Start slow and easy.
3. Set realistic exercise goals.
4. Find a support group.
5. Add variety.
6. Record your progress.

Exercising with Machines. The number of health clubs, commercial gyms, and fitness centers has risen dramatically in the past few years. There are an estimated fourteen thousand such facilities in the United States alone. Although going to a club or gym is not as convenient as working out at home, most offer variable-resistance machines that are too bulky or expensive for home use.

Whether variable-resistance machines develop strength faster or to a greater degree than free weights is still a matter of hot debate. Both methods of training have produced positive results. For people beginning a weight-training program, machines are usually easier to work with and safer to use than free weights.

In either case, you will have to experiment to find the right amount of weight you need for each exercise. Because working to muscular failure can be difficult and even painful, start out slowly, performing two or three sets at 80 or 90 percent of your maximum ability. For the first five or six sessions, keep the weight at levels you can lift comfortably for twelve to fifteen repetitions. Or if you do choose to work to failure, adjust the weight so that you can perform eight to twelve repetitions, stopping just short of failure, and then repeat each exercise two or three times. Your gains in strength will be greatest if you rest a few minutes before moving on to the next exercise. Try for two or three sessions a week.

WINNING
THE MENTAL GAME

You are bound to master the physical skills of archery long before the mental ones. When we get hooked on a new sport, we tend to concentrate exclusively on the muscular activities, which is appropriate. Only after finding your form and developing some shots can you begin to play the mental game. That is, first you learn to set up, aim, release, and follow through, and then you learn to "think" in archery.

And make no mistake, it is a thinking game. Even as a recreational shooter, mastering the so-called inner game of archery can give you a competitive advantage. If you mentally fortify yourself with the techniques in this chapter, you can become a better archer. In archery, as in all sports, strive for the three Cs: concentration, consistency, and confidence.

Confidence springs from consistency, and both are dependent on concentration.

CONCENTRATION

If you talk to accomplished athletes in any sport, you will hear them speak of the importance of concentration. Sometimes called focus, it's at the heart of success in any endeavor, especially archery.

Most everyone knows that concentration has to do with paying attention. Does that mean consciously willing yourself to focus? Is concentration a shrill voice in your head screaming over and over, "Pay attention!" until you do? Maybe at first.

Focus is delicate, elusive. Pay close attention to the trees and you may miss the forest, and vice versa. Eventually, if you stay with it, you will learn to relax and focus more naturally. Once you master the techniques and know when to use them, you may be able to turn game control over to your now well-developed instincts.

Your conscious mind, however, will want to interfere. Consider this athletic equation:

Performance = Potential – Interference

Performance is how well you actually do—your results; potential is a measurement of the best performance you are capable of at any given moment; interference is the mental static produced by the conscious mind. When pressure is minimal, the mind may become distracted: "Wonder where Donna is right now. . . . How about those Knicks! . . . I bet I look just like Robin Hood!"

As pressure mounts, so do self-doubts and anxiety, two other prime causes of mental static. Again, the conscious mind rushes in, usually to provide a litany of advice: "Deep breath . . . hold it now . . . eye on the target . . . smooth push and pull . . . whoops!"

With all that advice raining down on you, is it any wonder that you're tighter than last year's pants? And what happens when you're tight? The unwanted contraction of only a few extra muscle fibers in the arms is enough to force your arrow off-line, turning a potential bull's-eye into a weed burner.

A reduction of mental interference will improve performance, even with no change in potential (read: practice). In other words, get your head screwed on right, and you can become a better archer without even picking up a bow.

But the overactive conscious mind does not react well to being told to butt out. (It's rather like ordering yourself to sleep.) Instead, you will have to rely on deceit. Some coaches suggest distracting the conscious mind by focusing on something only marginally related to the task at hand. By giving it something else to chew on, the subconscious is left unfettered.

Three ways to distract that pesky conscious mind are by positive association, visualization, and shooting by the numbers. To associate positively, immerse yourself in positive recollections. Suppose you are shooting for the match. Like everyone, you've had both good and bad moments in the past. For best results, zero in on the successes and ignore the failures. Replay an imaginary tape that you might call "My Greatest Hits." Immerse yourself in positive recollections.

Visualization, first cousin to positive association, is a type of mental rehearsal in which you conjure up detailed visions of the activity before you do it. The first step in visualization is to relax. Use a method that works for you. You might close your eyes and take a few deep breaths, recite your favorite mantra, or play a mental videotape of a winning moment.

Focus on the finer points of the shot. See it as one fluid whole. Feel the fingers curled around the nock; hear the twang of the string's release, the zip of the arrow slicing through the air, the satisfying thump as it strikes the bull's-eye.

Visualization takes dedicated practice, but you can do it anywhere—in a bed or bathtub, at a bus stop—and the rewards can be staggering. Most top-flight athletes attribute some, if not most, of their success to visualization.

Research suggests that muscles respond to visualization of an act almost as if you were doing the act. Thus, the more intensely you visualize the perfect shot, the more entrenched it will be in your muscle memory. This kind of memory operates almost entirely on the subconscious level, which helps explain how you can make a great play but can't explain it to others.

The power of visualization received a lot of publicity in the seventies with the revelations of several famous athletes. Golfer Jack Nicklaus said that he never hit a shot without first seeing the ball's perfect flight followed by its "sitting up there high and white and pretty on the green." A successful shot, according to Nicklaus, was 50 percent visualization, 40 percent setup, and only 10 percent swing.

To shoot by the numbers, count to three each time you raise the bow, aim, and release. Recite "one" as you raise the bow, "two" as you do the push-pull, and "three" on the release and follow-through. Try to synchronize sound with event. It's harder than you think, and the conscious mind should be fully engaged in trying to accomplish it. Try it during practice and see if it works for you. You may find that counting "one, two, three . . . one, two, three" gives your shooting motion a rhythm it lacked.

ATTITUDE

The biggest difference between the competent and the excellent in any sport is mental preparation. Successful athletes find a way to remain calm or quickly regain their composure. To be effective, you must keep a check on counterproductive emotions. Some of us compete better than others when we're mad, but no one performs well in a rage. Analyze and try to correct missed shots, but don't dwell on them.

Judi Adams made the U.S. archery team in 1980 at age nineteen, but the Olympic boycott that year prevented her from competing. She missed making the team in 1984, '88, and '92, but in '96, as a thirty-six-year-old single mother, she made it back to the Olympic Games. Losing in the first round did not diminish her sense of accomplishment. Says Judi, "People think what's important is the gold, but it's the struggle."

HANDLING PRESSURE

As you improve and encounter better competition, the pressure mounts. It is often pressure that causes a great player to blow a shot he's made thousands of times before.

Picture this scenario: You're behind in a match against a pretty good local shooter. You need a bull's-eye to stay in the game. People are watching, and you feel the rivalry. Your guts are twisting like wet rope. Now that's pressure. Most everyone feels it at one time or another. The real question is whether you can control it. Successful people don't dodge pressure; they make it work to their benefit.

On the other hand, others seem to block it out entirely. Orlando Magic center Jon Koncak denied that having to replace the injured Shaquille O'Neal put pressure on him: "Pressure to me is being in an airplane and the pilot dies and they ask me to fly the plane."

SAFETY

•••

The safety principles of archery should be ingrained in your mind before you ever pick up a bow and arrow. Safety begins with the selection of proper equipment and clothing. It's best to wear a shirt or sweater that fits tightly around your chest and bow arm. Avoid sleeves that are so loose that they interfere with the bowstring. Wear shoes, even when practicing, to protect your feet should you step on an arrow hidden in the grass. Tie back long hair that might get caught in the bowstring. Wear an arm-guard and use a finger tab.

TARGET PLACEMENT AND MATERIALS

Safety should also be considered when selecting the shooting area and target materials. The placement of your target is of critical importance. Most people have enough sense to clear the area between the shooters and the target. Needless to say, don't shoot over roads, sidewalks, or child-care centers. Don't set up next to buildings or other obstacles that might shield someone approaching from the side. If you are inside, lock all doors between shooters and target so that no one will inadvertently walk in.

Try to create buffer zones around the target. Have plenty of room behind and beside the targets. Errant arrows can travel 30 yards or more beyond the target, so make sure there is a wide clear area extending at least 40 yards behind the target or place it in front of a steep dirt bank, which will stop arrows with no damage to them.

If you lack space, build a backstop. A piece of plywood protected by a mesh, cloth, or canvas curtain will serve you well. The curtain will catch the arrows, saving the tips and saving you the hassle of yanking them out of the wood. If you're inside, cover any windows behind the target with plywood.

Figure 28. Target backstop.

Curtain backstop

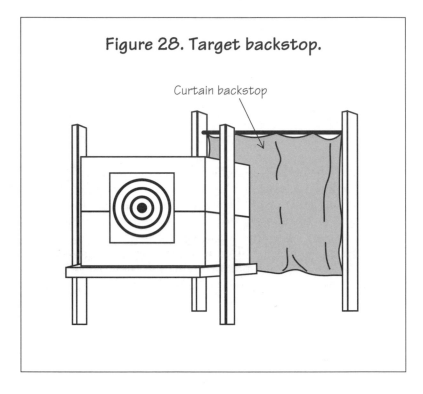

The ideal target material will stop a fast-moving arrow with no damage. Tightly baled straw, wood fiber, and excelsior all make excellent backstops, as long as they're covered to protect them from the weather. The best ones are made in a stationary baler and wrapped with two or three wires instead of twine. A simple grass mat on a portable stand can be both an indoor and an outdoor target. Ethafoam also does an excellent job of stopping arrows. It is more expensive than other materials, but it is lightweight, easy to move, suitable indoors and out, and doesn't need to be covered. Look for the type with a replaceable center core.

Some indoor clubs stack and compress layers of heavy cardboard, forming a target 20 to 24 inches thick. Archers shoot into the corrugated ends. When this target wears out, the cardboard layers can be taken apart, shuffled, and restacked, creating an almost new target.

Figure 29. Portable target stand.

Cardboard boxes and common agricultural hay bales are ineffective backstops. Most of your arrows will pass through them, making them both unsafe and hard on your arrows. Don't shoot broadhead points, used for hunting, at a target, except the ethafoam type with replaceable core. Broadheads will either cut the target to shreds or be impossible to remove.

EQUIPMENT SAFETY

Check your equipment before every practice session. Inspect arrows, bow limbs, cables, strings, and nocks for cracks, frays, and dents that might cause problems during shooting.

Evaluate each arrow point carefully, removing for repair any that are missing or loose. Cracked wooden arrow shafts are irreparable and should be broken in two and discarded. A cracked arrow that breaks at the moment the string is released can cause serious injury to the shooter, another archer, or a spectator. Bent aluminum arrows must be straightened before shooting so that they will fly straight and not damage the bow's arrow rest. Dented aluminum arrow shafts that are still straight can be shot, though perhaps with less accuracy than usual. Most such dents cannot be fixed. Also check your arrows' nocks and discard any that are cracked. A cracked nock can slip off the string before release.

Bows, too, must be checked carefully. Frayed strings and cables can break and cause injury. Check the serving on your bowstring; if it is unraveling, have it re-served or replace the entire string. Limbs rarely develop cracks, but when they do, they are potentially dangerous. A cracked limb could break at full draw and cause an injury.

If you are shooting with a recurve bow, check the brace height. Make sure it's at least 6 inches, lest the bowstring slap your wrist.

Inspect compound bows to confirm that the steel cables are securely attached to the bowstring and properly routed on the pulleys.

Even equipment in good working order can be unsafe if it's not right for you. For example, an arrow too short for the archer can fall off the arrow rest and cause serious injury to the shooter's hand or to someone else. Or it can lodge between the string and the bow handle, damaging the bow. Have an instructor or pro shop salesperson verify that your equipment is a good match.

SAFE SHOOTING

When you shoot with others, make sure everyone understands the basic safety rules:

- All archers should take their positions on the shooting line when instructed to do so. They should straddle the mark so that everyone is in a straight line. No shooter should be in front of or behind anyone else.
- A designated starter should signal the start and finish of the shooting round. Nock your first arrow only after the signal to shoot is given.
- Know the signals. In tournaments, one whistle blast signals the start of shooting, two blasts the end of shooting, and three or more blasts means a halt to shooting because of an emergency.

Figure 30. Shooting line.

- Nock your arrow only at the nock locator.
- Point a nocked arrow only at the ground or at the target. An arrow released from even a partially drawn bow can cause injury.
- No one should start toward the target until the shooting has stopped and the starter has given the all-clear signal.

- If you drop an arrow or other piece of equipment in front of the shooting line while shooting is in progress, don't step out to get it. Instead, use your bow to drag it back to the line. If you can't reach it, leave it there until the shooting has stopped.
- Never shoot an arrow at anything other than the target, especially straight up into the air. Shooting at tin cans thrown in the air is not appropriate on a normal target line.

After shooting, the following safety rules should be observed:

- During a timed shooting period, shooters finishing before others should step back from the line. If the shooters right next to you are at full draw, however, wait until they release.
- Leave your bow in a bow rack or in a designated area before retrieving your arrows. Someone could trip over a bow left on the ground or floor.
- Wait for the all-clear signal (two whistle blasts) before you walk to the target to locate your arrows. Don't run; you could fall and pierce yourself with an arrow.
- Retrieve the short arrows first as you walk to the target. If the fletching is embedded, pull the arrow forward to avoid damaging the fletching.
- When pulling out arrows in the target, make sure nobody is behind you. Pull out the top ones before the bottom ones. If you bend over to pull out the bottom arrows first, the upper arrows may stab you in the face. Place one hand flat against the target face to prevent it from ripping, then grasp the arrow shaft close to the target with the other hand. Twist the arrow back and forth to remove it.
- If you need to go behind the target to locate an arrow, have someone stand in front of the target to prevent others from shooting the next round. If you are hunting arrows alone, it's a good idea to prop your bow against the target in plain sight to deter anyone from shooting. If others are waiting for you to find your arrows, spend only a few minutes hunting. You can search more thoroughly after the last round.

Finding lost arrows can be a challenge. Sometimes a rake can be useful. A long stick with a bent nail in the end makes a great arrow rake. Drag the rake in a line perpendicular to the flight of the arrow at intervals of about 2 feet. Sometimes an arrow can skip quite a distance and not be where you think it is. Other times it can deflect wildly and be lost forever.

Archery is usually quite a safe sport. It is the careless archer who is sometimes unsafe, typically out of ignorance. Reread this chapter and make safety a habit, just as you make nocking, drawing, aiming, and releasing a habit.

ARCHERY GAMES

....

TARGET ARCHERY

Target archery is the sport of shooting arrows over distances ranging from 30 to 90 meters (33 to 99 yards).

CLOUT SHOOTING

The origins of clout shooting lie in a medieval military practice.
The archers, known as "the artillery," were used in battle to attack
the enemy at long range. In practice, they shot at a piece of cloth,
called a clout, at 180 yards or more.

On the ground, lay out a target 48 feet in diameter, with concentric circles drawn in proportion to the standard target face (48
inches), at a ratio of 1 foot to 1 inch. Place a 5-foot stake in the center of the target, with a balloon or flag tied to the top.

Archers shoot from an agreed-upon distance (tournament distances are 120 and 140 yards for women, 180 yards for men). The
whole group shoots at the same time, with six arrows making an
end. Shooting may be either one-way or two-way with a target at
each end. Scoring, determined by the position of the arrow tip, is
the same as for a standard target: gold, 9; red, 7; blue, 5; black, 3;
white, 1.

ARCHERY GOLF

This game can be played on a regulation golf course or on a spe-
cially designed archery golf course, several of which exist around
the country.

The rules of archery golf are similar to those of golf, except that the goal of each "hole" is to hit a cardboard disk or a cloth ball target by the side of each green. The archer who takes the least number of shots to get around the course is the winner.

Here are some other common rules:

- Each group shall select a captain to make decisions and to record scores after leaving each green.
- Each competitor may use only one bow unless it breaks, in which case the shot may be repeated with another bow and no penalty. The same is true of a broken bowstring.
- Participants may use arrows of any type, although typically three arrows are needed: a flight arrow, an approach arrow, and a putting arrow (generally a flu-flu with a spike tip).
- Each shot and each penalty counts one stroke.
- The stand for a field or approach shot must be directly behind the landing point of the previous shot.
- The archer with the lowest score on the previous hole shoots first on the next one.
- After the tee shots, the archer farthest from the target shoots first. Other archers should not advance until the shot is completed.
- The bow may be held in any position, and full draw is not required.
- An arrow in an unplayable lie may be shot from a point of equal or greater distance from the target, with a penalty of one stroke added.
- A lost arrow, if not found in five minutes, must be replaced. The new arrow should be shot from a location agreed upon by the group, with a penalty of one stroke.
- If an arrow lands so close to the target that the archer, in his stance behind the spot where the point of the previously shot arrow landed, can touch it with the point of the nocked arrow, the shot may be conceded.
- The target may be turned to face the shooting archer.

BIRD SHOOTING

You will need half a dozen cardboard disks (homemade or purchased) and a range that is safely clear for about 100 yards. One person throws a disk up and about 10 yards in front of the shooters, who are standing with arrows nocked and bows ready. Increase the distance as archers become more accurate. Shoot as teams or with one member from each team shooting at a time. The team with the most hits after a specified number of throws, or after a specified time, wins.

Variation: Release balloons along the ground for rabbit shooting. Score the same way as for bird shooting. You may want to use blunt arrow tips.

BINGO

Construct a simulated bingo card on a target face, and shoot from an agreed-upon distance. The first person or team to hit five squares in a line in any direction wins.

TIC-TAC-TOE

On each target, place nine balloons in three rows of three balloons each. Shoot from an agreed-upon distance, usually 15 yards. The first person or team to break three balloons in line in any direction wins.

Variation: At the end of the tic-tac-toe game, keep shooting; the first team to break every balloon is the winner.

SWINGING BALL

Suspend a soft rubber ball on a 2-foot string from the top of a target. One person sets the ball in motion and then gets safely out of the way before the archers, shooting from an agreed-upon distance, are allowed to draw. Score 2 points when the ball is pinned and 1 point when it is struck but not pinned. Play to an agreed-upon score.

WAND SHOOTING

Place a strip of masking tape vertically on the target face from top to bottom. Shooting from 15 yards, score a point each time someone hits the tape. Compete individually or in teams, and play to an agreed-upon score.

WILLIAM TELL

Set up a target depicting a boy with an apple on his head. Shooting from 15 yards away, the first team to hit the apple is the winner. Eliminate any team member who hits the pictured boy.

RULES OF
COMPETITIVE ARCHERY

··

Excerpts selected from the
International Archery Federation

7.1   RANGE LAYOUT

7.1.1   Outdoor Target Archery Rounds

7.1.1.1.   Tolerance on field dimensions at 90/70/60 meters shall be
+ 30cm; at 50/30 meters +15cm.

7.1.1.2.   A Waiting Line shall be indicated at least five meters
behind the shooting line.

7.1.1.3   Each buttress shall be numbered and set up at an angle
of about 15 degrees from the vertical.

7.1.1.4   The center of the gold shall be 130cm above the ground
as measured from an estimated even ground level. When
using multiple faces (3 or 4) the center(s) of the upper
face(s) shall be 160cm above ground level, the centers of
the lower faces shall be about 42cm below the upper
face(s). For FITA Championships the triangular symmet-
rical arrangement of the three centers is mandatory. A
tolerance measurement shall not exceed +5cm. The
height of the centers of the gold in a line of buttresses on
the range should at all times look straight.

7.1.2.   Indoor Target Archery Rounds

7.1.2.1   The range shall be squared off and each distance accurately measured from a point vertically beneath the gold
of each target to the shooting line. Tolerance on range
dimensions shall be +10cm at 25/18 meters.

7.1.2.3   The buttress may be set up at any angle between vertical
and about 15 degrees from the vertical, but a line of buttresses shall be set up all at the same angle. Each buttress shall be numbered.

7.1.3 Field Archery Rounds

7.1.3.1 The course shall be arranged so that the shooting posts and the targets can be reached without undue difficulty, hazard or waste of time.

7.1.3.2 The targets as described in Article 6.4.3 shall be laid out in such order as to allow maximum variety and best use of the terrain.

7.1.4 Flight

7.1.4.1 The Base Line or Shooting Line from which the arrows are shot, and from which the measurements are made, shall be at least 20 meters long.

7.1.4.2 The Range Line, which is at right angles to the Shooting Line, must be clearly marked by stakes from zero to 100 meters beyond the existing record. From zero to 300 meters, the stakes will be every 100 meters. From 300 meters to the end of the range line, the stakes shall be every 25 meters.

7.1.4.3 The landing area, defined as any ground on which the arrows are expected to land, must be at least 200 meters wide. This area must be free of obstructions and hazards, such as trees, buildings, fences, ditches, etc., and should provide turf (ground) favorable for arrows to land on. The landing area should stretch back from the end of the range line towards the base at least 450 meters.

7.2 VENUE EQUIPMENT

7.2.1 Outdoor Target Archery Rounds

7.2.1.1 Target Faces
There are three FITA Outdoor Target Faces, 122cm and 80cm in diameter and 80cm multiple face.

- Description
122cm and 80cm faces are divided into five concentric color zones arranged from the center outward as follows:

Gold (Yellow), Red, Light Blue, Black, and White. Each color is in turn divided by a thin line into two zones of equal width thus making ten scoring zones of equal width measured from the center of the Gold:

- 6.1cm on the 122cm target face;
- 4cm on the 80cm target face.

Such dividing lines, and any dividing lines which may be used between colors, shall be made entirely within the higher scoring zones in each case. Any line marking the outermost edge of the White shall be made entirely within the scoring zone. The width of the thin dividing line as well as the outermost line shall not exceed 2mm on either the 122cm or the 80cm target faces. The center of the target face is termed the "pinhole" and shall be indicated by a small "x" (cross) the lines of which shall not exceed 1mm in width and 4mm in length. For the Compound Division an inner ten (10) ring 6.1cm in diameter for the 122cm target face and 4cm in diameter for the 80cm target face is required.

Scoring Values and Color Specifications

Scoring Values	Colors
10	Gold
9	Gold
8	Red
7	Red
6	Light Blue
5	Light Blue
4	Black
3	Black
2	White
1	White

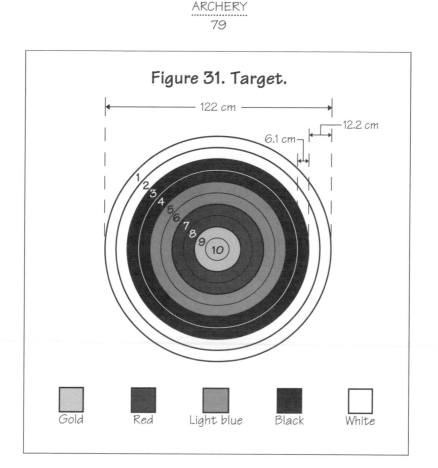

Figure 31. Target.

- Material of Target Faces
  Target Faces may be made of paper, cloth or any other suitable material. All faces shall be uniform and of the same material.

7.2.1.2 Buttresses

The size of the buttress front, whether round or square, must not be less than 124cm in any direction to ensure that any arrow hitting buttress and just missing the outermost edge of the target remain in the buttress. Buttresses shall be pegged securely to the ground to prevent them from being blown over by wind. Any portion of a buttress and of its support likely to damage an arrow shall be covered.

7.2.2 Indoor Target Archery Rounds

7.2.2.1 Target Faces

There are six FITA Indoor Target faces:

- 60cm diameter face;
- 60cm triangular triple face;
- 60cm vertical triple face;
- 40cm diameter face;
- 40cm triangular triple face;
- 40cm vertical triple face;

  Only those Indoor Target Faces produced by a manufacturer licensed by FITA shall be used at all FITA competitions.

- Description

  The 60cm and 40cm faces are divided by a thin line into five concentric color zones arranged from the center outward as follows: Gold (Yellow), Red, Light Blue, Black, and White. Each color is in turn divided by a thin line into two zones of equal width thus making all ten scoring zones of equal width measured from the center of the gold:

    - 3cm on the 60cm target face.
    - 2cm on the 40cm target face.

  Such dividing lines, and any dividing lines which may be used between colors, shall be made entirely within the higher zone in each case. Any line marking the outermost edge of the white shall be made entirely within the scoring zone. The width of the thin dividing lines as well as the outermost line shall not exceed 2mm on both the 60cm and 40cm target faces. The center of the target face is termed the "pinhole" and shall be indicated by a small cross "x" the lines of which shall not exceed 1mm in width and 4mm in length.

  For the Compound Division an inner ten (10) ring of 3cm in diameter for the 60cm target faces and 2cm in diameter for the 40cm target faces is required. In addition triple faces as follows may be used. They have the same dimensions as the FITA 60cm and 40cm faces respectively, but with the 5 to 1 scoring zones removed. The lowest scoring zone is therefore Light Blue 6. Each set consists of three small faces on a white background arranged symmetrically in a triangular pattern with the centers respectively bottom left, at the apex, and at the bottom right or in a vertical row. The centers of the golds shall be approximately 32cm distant from each other on 60cm faces and 22cm distant from each other on 40cm faces.

7.2.2.2. Buttresses

- The size of the buttress face, whether round or square, must be large enough to ensure that any arrow hitting the buttress and just missing the outside of the target face, remains in the buttress;

- Any portion of the buttress and its support likely to damage an arrow shall be covered. Care is necessary, particularly when more than one target face is placed on the buttress, that arrows passing through the buttress are not damaged by the support....

7.2.3   Field Archery Rounds

7.2.3.1   For the Unmarked and Marked courses; the FITA Field Face shall be used. Only those FITA Field faces produced by a manufacturer licensed by FITA shall be used at FITA competitions.

The FITA Field Face consists of a yellow center spot and four equal scoring zones.

The background of the face shall be white. The five ring scoring zone (spot) for the Compound Division (inner 5) is yellow. The five ring scoring zone for the Olympic and Barebow Divisions is of the same yellow. The two (2) scoring zones shall be divided by a black line of maximum 1mm in width. The rest of the face shall be black. The four scoring zones shall be divided by white lines of maximum 1mm in width. Any dividing lines shall be in the higher scoring zones. In the center of the spot there shall be a fine lined X.

7.2.3.2   Of the FITA Field Faces, there are four sizes:

DIMENSIONS OF FACES

Color of Zones	Scoring Value Points	0 20cm Sizes of Zones in cm	0 40cm Sizes of Zones in cm	0 60cm Sizes of Zones in cm	0 80cm Sizes of Zones in cm	Tolerances in ± mm
yellow	5**	0 2	0 4	0 6	0 8	1
yellow	5*	0 4	0 8	0 12	0 16	1
black	4 All	0 8	0 16	0 24	0 32	1
black	3 All	0 12	0 24	0 36	0 48	3
black	2 All	0 16	0 32	0 48	0 64	3
black	1 All	0 20	0 40	0 60	0 80	3

0 = Diameter   *Olympic and Barebow   **Compound

7.2.3.3   In the FITA Forest Round, picture faces may be used as set forth below:

DIAMETER OF INNER RING

07.5/5cm	015/10cm	022.5/15cm	030/20cm
	Typical Animals, such as:		
Squirrel	Hare	Roedeer	Bear
Rabbit	Fox	Wolverine	Deer
Marten	Raccoon	Wolf	Wild Boar
Woodcock	Woodgrouse		

The Forest Round target faces consist of pictures (photograph/drawing/painting) of animals (see chart) with such colors and contrast that people with normal eyesight can see them clearly under normal daylight conditions at the relevant distances. The pictures should be printed on a white background. The picture faces have two (2) concentric inner rings and an outer ring/line. The smaller inner ring is the Compound scoring zone, the larger inner ring is the scoring zone for the Barebow and the Olympic Divisions. The outer ring corresponds to the animal's body contour if this is clear, otherwise there shall be a clear line closely following the body contour. The outer ring/line is the same for all Divisions. Organizers may use 3-D animal figures instead of or in addition to animal faces. However, the Organizer must clearly advise the competitors of this fact in the invitation since 3-D animal figures do not comply with Article 7.1.3.7.

7.2.4   Clout

7.2.4.1   The Clout target shall be circular, 15 meters in diameter and shall be divided into five concentric scoring zones arranged from the center outward and each measuring 1.5 meters in width. Each dividing line shall be entirely within the higher scoring zone.

7.2.4.2   The Clout target may be marked out on the ground, or the scoring lines may be determined by a steel tape or non-stretch cord marked off at the dividing lines.

7.2.4.3   The center of the Clout target shall be marked by a brightly colored distinctive triangular flag: the CLOUT. This flag shall not measure more than 80cm in length and 30cm in width. The flag is to be affixed to a round pole of softwood, firmly fixed vertically in the ground, so that the lower edge of the flag shall not be more than 50cm from the ground.

7.2.4.4   The values of each scoring zone of the Clout target from the center outward are: 5 − 4 − 3 − 2 − 1.

7.3.1   Competitors' Equipment: General Regulations

7.3.1.2   Standard Bow Equipment
FITA Standard Bow Equipment is defined as follows:
- The bow shall be of a simple design, either take-apart (with wooden or metal riser) or of one-piece construction.

In both cases the limbs shall be of wooden and/or fiberglass construction.

- The bowstring material may not be of a higher specification than Dacron.
- The arrowrest shall be of a simple, flexible or rigid design and it shall be non-adjustable. A simple non-adjustable pressure point may be used but shall be placed no further back than 2cm from the throat (pivot point) of the handle.
- Arrows shall not exceed a specification of XX75 or equivalent, shall be of equivalent price range and performance. The nocks shall be of simple construction, either conical or insert fitting. The points shall be conical or oval in shape. The vanes shall be of soft plastic material or of natural feathers.
- Finger protection shall not include any form of stiffening or locating platform or similar device or any device to help hold, draw and release the string.

7.3.1.3 For the Compound Division, the following equipment is permitted.

- A Compound Bow, where the draw is mechanically varied by a system of pulleys and/or cams. The peak draw weight must not exceed 60lbs. The bow is braced for use by either a single bowstring attached directly between the two string nocks of the bow limbs, eccentric wheels or attached to the bow cables, as may be applicable to the particular design. Cable guards are permitted.
- A bowstring of any number of strands of the material chosen for the purpose, with a center serving to accommodate the drawing fingers or release aid. A nocking point may be fitted to which may be added serving(s) to fit the arrow nock as necessary. To locate this point nock locators may be fitted. In addition attachments are permitted on the string to serve as a lip or nose mark, a peep-hole, a peep-hole 'hold-in-line' device, etc.
- An arrowrest which can be adjustable, any moveable pressure button, pressure point or arrow plate, may all be used on the bow provided that they are not electric or electronic. The pressure point shall be placed no further

than 6cm back (inside) from the throat of the handle (pivot point of the bow).

8.3   SCORING

8.3.1   Outdoor Target Archery Rounds

8.3.1.10 An arrow shall be scored according to the position of the shaft in the target face. Should the shaft of an arrow touch two colors, or touch any dividing lines between two scoring zones, that arrow shall score the higher value of the zones affected.

8.3.1.11 Should a fragment of a target face be missing, including a dividing line or where two colors meet, or if the dividing line is displaced by an arrow, then an imaginary circular line shall be used for judging the value of any arrow that may hit such a part.

8.3.1.12 Unless all arrow holes are suitably marked on each occasion when arrows are scored and drawn from the target, arrows rebounding from or passing completely through the buttress shall not be scored.

8.3.1.14 An arrow hitting:
- The target and rebounding shall score according to its impact on the target provided that all arrow holes have been marked and an unmarked hole or mark can be identified;
- The target and hanging from it, shall have the competitor or competitors on the target stop shooting and signal with a flag. When shooting of that end has been completed by the other competitors on the line, a judge with the competitor shall note the value of the arrow, remove it, make the hole and place the arrow behind the target...
- The target and passing completely through the buttress, provided all arrow holes have been marked and provided an unmarked hole can be identified, shall score according to the value of the hole in the target face;
- Another arrow in the nock and remaining embedded therein, shall score according to the value of the arrow struck;

- Another arrow, and then hitting the target face after deflection, shall score as it lies in the target face;
- Another arrow, and then rebounding, shall score the value of the struck arrow, provided the damaged arrow can be identified.

8.3.2 Indoor Target Archery Rounds

Parameters outlined in Article 8.3.1 (Scoring for Outdoor Target Archery Rounds) are applicable for Indoor Target Archery Rounds.

8.3.3 Field Archery Rounds

8.3.3.6 Parameters outlined in Article 8.3.1.10. apply to scoring in like circumstances in Field Archery Rounds

8.3.3.7 Parameters outlined in Article 8.3.1.11. apply to scoring in like circumstances in Field Archery Rounds

8.3.3.9 Unless all arrows are suitably marked on each occasion when arrows are scored and drawn from the target, arrows rebounding from or passing completely through the target buttress shall not be scored except as follows:

- If all of the competitors on that shooting group agree on the value of the arrow that has rebounded from or passed through the target buttress, that arrow shall be given the agreed upon value;
- If all of the competitors in that shooting group agree that an arrow has rebounded from or passed through the target buttress, but cannot agree on the value of the arrow, then the arrow shall be given the value of the lowest unmarked arrow hole that is found on the target face;
- If all of the competitors in that shooting group cannot agree that an arrow has rebounded from or passed through the target buttress, then that arrow shall not be scored.

8.3.3.10 An arrow hitting:

- Another arrow in the nock and remaining embedded therein shall score according to the value of the arrow struck;

- Another arrow, and then hitting the target face after deflection, shall score as it lies in the target;
- Another arrow, and then rebounding shall score the value of the arrow struck, provided the damaged arrow can be identified.

8.3.4   Clout

8.3.4.4   The value of the arrows that do not stick in the ground shall be determined by the position of their points as they lie.

8.3.4.5   Arrows sticking in the CLOUT, or in the pole, shall score five.

8.3.4.6   No competitor, except the appointed arrow gatherers, shall enter the Clout target until his name has been called to record the value of his arrows.

8.3.5   Scoring (Flight)

8.3.5.1   Distance measurements shall be made with a steel tape along the range line. The distance shot shall be measured to that point on the range line at which a line at right angles to the range line passes through the point where the arrow enters the ground; the line should pass through the pile end of the arrow.

8.3.5.5   To facilitate scoring, the scorer stands beside the competitor's longest shot as only the competitor's longest shot is recorded.

GLOSSARY

∙∙∙

actual draw length: the arrow length needed by an archer, measured from the bottom of the slit of the arrow nock to the back of the bow.

address: to assume the proper stance preparatory to shooting an arrow.

aim: to visually align an arrow tip or bow sight aperture with a target.

alignment: relationship of eye to string and string to bow at full draw.

American round: a sequence of shots that consists of thirty arrows shot from 60 yards, thirty arrows from 50 yards, and thirty arrows from 40 yards.

anchor point: the spot under the chin, on the jaw, or on the side of the face to which the archer draws the bowstring while aiming.

archer's paradox: the bending, and then stabilizing, of the arrow as it leaves the bow, created by the force of the string on the arrow.

archery golf: a game played on a golf course or a spe-cially designed course with bow and arrow, using a golf scoring system.

armguard: leather or plastic device worn on the inside of the bow forearm to protect from string sting.

arrow: the principal missile shot from a bow. Most arrows are 22 to 30 inches in length, with the choice determined mostly by the user's arm length. There are five types of arrows: target, field, hunting, flight and fishing.

arrow case: a box, usually of wood, in which arrows are kept.

arrowhead: the striking end of an arrow, usually made of steel. Ancient heads were of flint and bronze, and some primitive people continue to use heads made of hardwood, horn, and bone.

arrow plate: a piece of leather glued to the bow above the arrow rest to protect the bow.

arrow rest: a small shelf fixed on newer bows that takes the place of the knuckle as a resting spot for the arrow.

arrowsmith: a maker of iron arrows. After tempering or case-hardening the arrows, the smith turned them over to the fletcher, who assembled the complete arrow.

arrow straightener: a mechanical device for detecting and eliminating bends in aluminum arrows.

artificial point of aim: in target archery, a mark placed on the ground between the shooting line and the target at which to aim, instead of using a bow sight or mark on the bow.

back: the part of the bow away from the archer.

backed bow: bow with a protective covering of rawhide or fiberglass on the back.

barebow: in field archery, a shooting classification indicating that the archer may not use a sighting device of any kind on the bow.

bare shaft: an arrow shaft with no fletching.

blunt: a flat arrow tip used for small-game hunting.

bolt: a crossbow arrow, usually 14 to 16 inches long.

bounce out: an arrow that strikes the scoring area of the target but doesn't stick.

bow: an instrument consisting of a handle, riser, and two flexible limbs each ending in a tip with a string nock. The potential energy created by the archer in drawing the string against the resistance of the two flexible limbs is converted to kinetic energy when the string is released, giving velocity to the arrow.

bow arm: the arm that lifts and supports the bow during shooting.

bow bracer: a device used to brace, or string, a bow.

bowhunter: in field archery, a shooting classification in which the archer uses hunting-weight arrows and simple pin sights.

bow scale: a mechanical device that measures the draw weight of a bow at any stage of the draw.

bow sight: a mechanical device attached to the bow to help the archer aim.

bow sling: a leather strap attached to the bow that allows the archer's hand to remain in contact with the bow without gripping it.

bow square: a device that attaches to the bowstring and lies on the arrow rest to measure brace height and nocking-point location.

bow stave: piece of wood from which a bow is made.

bowstring: the string of a bow, usually made of Dacron or Kevlar.

bow stringer: a device used to brace, or string, a bow. Also called a *bow bracer.*

bow window: a cutout section above the grip of a bow. Also called *sight window.*

bowyer: a bow designer and maker.

brace: to string a bow.

brace height: when the bow is strung, the distance between the pivot point of the bow and the string. Also called *string height.*

broadhead: a sharp, triangular metal arrowhead used for hunting.

brush button: a soft rubber object set at each end of the bowstring to dampen bow noise.

bull's-eye: the area on the target face having the highest scoring value, usually the center.

butt: the target backstop, made of grass, excelsior, straw, cardboard, polyethylene, foam, or fiber.

cant: tilt of the bow to the left or right while shooting.

cast: the speed and distance a bow can propel an arrow.

chest protector: nylon netting or vinyl worn over the clothing to prevent the bowstring from catching.

clicker: metal device attached to the side of the bow above the arrow rest that acts as a draw check. The arrow is placed under the metal strip and drawn, and a clicking sound alerts the archer when the draw is complete.

closed stance: shooting stance in which the line to the target runs from the tip of the back foot through the ball of the front foot to the center of the target.

clout: long-distance shooting event that uses a 48-foot target set flat on the ground.

cock feather: the odd-colored feather positioned at a right angle to the string. Also known as the *index feather.*

collapse: an error in form in which the archer eases up at release, losing muscle control.

Columbian round: a competitive round in which archers shoot twenty-four arrows at each of three distances: 50, 40, and 30 yards.

composite bow: a bow made of three or more layers of dissimilar materials. (Contrasted with *laminated bow.*)

compound bow: bow utilizing a cable system with an eccentric pulley at each limb tip. Because it stores energy and produces peak resistance at middraw and a dropoff in resistance beyond that point, the archer thus has a hold weight less than the actual draw weight of the bow.

creeping: letting the drawing hand—and thus the arrow— ease forward before release.

crest: the identifying marks on the arrow, usually bands near the fletching.

crossbow: a weapon formed by fastening a bow at right angles to a stock or tiller. It can be aimed and shot like a gun.

dead release: releasing the string by allowing the string fingers to relax rather than by moving the drawing hand.

down wind: a wind that blows from the archer toward the target.

draw: to pull the bowstring back into full anchor position.

draw check: determining how much of the arrow has been drawn prior to a shot.

draw home: to draw an arrow fully so that it is ready for release.

drawing arm: the arm that draws back the bowstring.

drawing fingers: the middle three fingers of the drawing hand.

draw length: a measure at full draw from the back of the bow to the bottom of the slot in the arrow nock.

draw weight: the amount of energy in pounds required to draw a bow a specified distance, usually 28 inches.

dress shield: a triangular piece of leather, plastic, or other material, fitted with straps, to prevent the archer's clothing, from shoulder to chest, from catching on the bowstring when it is released.

drift: deflection of an arrow from its intended path due to a crosswind.

dry release: release of the drawn bowstring without an arrow, which can cause serious damage to a bow.

dynabow: a compound bow with a cam on one bow tip but no eccentric pulley on the other.

eccentric pulley: a round wheel mounted at the limb tip, used to lessen the amount of weight held on the bowstring at full draw.

efficiency: a measure of bow quality, specifically energy output over energy input, expressed as a percentage.

end: a specified number of arrows shot at one time or position prior to scoring and retrieval.

face: the part of the bow facing the shooter; also called *belly*. Also, the front of the target.

field archery: a type of archery shot in terrain ranging from open fields to thick brush. It is shot up hills and down, over creeks and ponds, from bridges and gullies. It can be enjoyed anywhere a target can be placed outdoors.

field arrow: an arrow with a long, tapered point, used outside for field archery.

field captain: man in charge of a tournament.

field point: an arrow point that is heavier than a target point and similar in weight to a broadhead. It can be unscrewed from an aluminum arrow.

finger sling: a piece of leather, plastic, or rope looped at each end, through which the archer slips the thumb and a finger, permitting a loose grip of the bow.

finger tab: a flat piece of leather that fits over the three fingers that hold the bowstring. A finger tab protects the fingers from the string and allows for a smoother release.

fishtailing: a back-and-forth movement of the nock end of an arrow in flight.

FITA: Federation Internationale de Tir à l'Arc (International Target Archery Federation), an organization that conducts world championships for archers using the recurve bow.

fletcher: an arrow maker.

fletching: the feathers or plastic vanes near the nock end of arrows. These guide and stabilize the arrow in flight.

flight: a competitive round of shooting for distance. Also, the path of an arrow.

flight compensator: metal object placed under the stabilizers to counter any torque caused by the archer.

flight shooting: a form of archery in which the object is to shoot an arrow the greatest distance possible.

flinch: sudden body movement at full draw caused by indecision or a desire to release too soon.

flu-flu: an arrow with large fletching mounted in a continuous spiral, sometimes used for wing shooting. Though the fletching allows normal flight at first, the extra wind drag soon slows the arrow, usually within 50 to 60 yards.

follow-through: the holding of the release position to assure smooth accuracy.

foot marker: anything used to mark the exact position of the feet at address so that the archer can duplicate his footwork on subsequent shots.

freestyle: in field archery, a shooting style that allows the use of any kind of hand-held bow with the accessories of the archer's choice.

full draw: the position the archer assumes just before release, with the bowstring pulled back and the draw hand anchored near the face or neck.

gap shooting: a method of aiming in which the archer estimates the shooting distance from the arrow tip to the target.

gold: the center of the target.

gold fever: the inability to hold the bow sight in the bull's-eye.

grain: unit of arrow weight.

grip: the part of the bow handle where the archer places the bow hand.

ground quiver: a metal rod stuck in the ground, designed to hold bows and arrows for the archer on the range.

grouping: the cluster or strike pattern of a series of arrows.

handicap: the number of artificial points an archer receives.

handicap differential: the difference between an archer's scratch score and perfect.

handle riser: the center part of the bow, exclusive of the limbs. Originally, the riser was a short piece of wood glued to the belly of the grip of a wooden bow to reinforce the center section and to give a better fit to the hand.

hanging arrow: an arrow that has penetrated the target with the tip only and hangs down across the target face.

head: the tip, point, or pile of the arrow.

heeling: a shooting flaw in which the archer suddenly pushes forward with the heel of the bow hand.

hen feathers: the two feathers that lie next to the string and on either side of the cock feather. The two hen feathers are usually the same color but different from that of the cock feather.

high anchor: an anchor position in which the draw hand contacts the side of the face.

high wrist: shooting position in which the top of the wrist is held in line with the top of the bow arm. More tension is placed on wrist muscles than in other wrist positions.

hit: a shot that lands within the scoring area of a target face.

holding: maintaining an arrow at full draw while aiming.

IBO: International Bowhunting Organization.

index feather: see *cock feather.*

instability: said of a bow that has design flaws that exaggerate small errors of form, turning them into major faults.

jerking: pulling the drawing hand sharply backward or down as the arrow is released.

jig: a device for putting feathers on arrows. Also, one for making strings.

kick: recoil of the bow upon release.

kisser button: a plastic device with a center hole that attaches to the string. It contacts the lips when in the correct anchor position, assuring a more consistent draw.

Kyudo: "the way of the bow." The formal Japanese art of archery that adheres to traditional methods and techniques. It is a branch of Zen Buddhism in which the physical and mental disciplines of the bow and arrow are used as aids in achieving a spiritual goal.

lady paramount: woman in charge of a tournament.

laminated bow: layered bow made from several layers of basically similar materials bonded together to take advantage of the best features of each. (Contrasted with *composite bow.*)

letdown: a return to the ready position without releasing the bowstring.

level: a small fluid level attached to the bow that helps the archer maintain a vertical bow position.

limbs: the arms of a bow, above and below the handle riser.

limited: in field archery, a shooting style in which the archer must draw and release the bowstring with the fingers.

longbow: a bow with no recurve, popular in England during the Middle Ages. Although not as efficient as a recurve bow, the longbow doesn't require the bonding together of materials, which was a daunting task in damp, ol' England.

loops: the woven or served bends in the ends of a bowstring that fit into the limb notches when the bow is braced. Also called *eyes.*

loose: antiquated term meaning to release the string.

low wrist: shooting position in which the hand is placed flat against the bow handle, with pressure flowing directly into the forearm.

mass weight: the physical weight of the bow, including accessories.

match: a competitive event.

midnock: a nock tapered down from the base to the groove, providing a smoother release.

misnock: a mistake that occurs when the string is not in the nock of the arrow at release, and the arrow falls from the bow instead of flying toward the target.

NAA: National Archery Association, the organization in the United States responsible for selecting and training men's and women's archery teams for the Olympics, world championships, and Pan-Am Games.

net score: an archer's score after his scratch score has been adjusted by his handicap.

NFAA: National Field Archery Association, the governing body for field archery in the United States.

nock: the grooved plastic piece at the back end of the arrow into which the string is placed; the act of placing the arrow on the bowstring; or one of the grooves at each limb tip that hold the bowstring in position.

nock end: the end of the arrow that fits against the string.

nocking point: a specific spot on the string where the nock locator, and hence the arrow, is placed.

nockset locator: a stop, usually a small metal ring around the bowstring against which the arrow is placed. Its purpose is to fix a position on the bowstring at which the nock of the arrow can be placed prior to every shot.

notch: the slot at the end of the limb tip of a recurve bow into which the bowstring is seated.

open stance: shooting stance in which a straight line to the target runs through the middle of the back foot and the toes of the front foot.

overbowed: said of an archer using a bow heavier than he can draw, hold, and shoot continuously with good form.

overdraw: to draw so far that the point of the arrow passes the face of the bow. Also, to draw a bow beyond its safe limits.

overshoot: to shoot above and beyond the target.

overstrung: said of a bow braced with too short a string, making the brace height too high.

PAA: the Professional Archers' Association, which oversees competition for professional archers.

pass-through: an arrow that goes completely through the target. Because it can be difficult to score such an arrow, a predetermined scoring value is usually assigned to pass-throughs.

peak weight: the highest weight achieved during the draw of a compound bow.

peeking: an error by the archer in which he tilts his head right or left of the string to watch the arrow in flight.

peep sight: a small aperture tied into the bowstring to allow the archer to look through the hole and line up the bow sight and target.

perfect end: shooting all six arrows in the bull's-eye for a score of 54.

petticoat: the edge of the target outside the scoring area.

pile: the tip, head, or point of the arrow.

pinching: squeezing the nock of the arrow with the draw fingers during the draw.

pin sight: a simple but effective sight, consisting of a flat metal plate with slots into which a series of sight pins can be attached.

pivot point: the spot on the bow's grip that is farthest from the string.

point: the arrow tip.

point-of-aim: a method of aiming in which the arrow point is aligned with some point either below or above the target.

point weight: a measure, in grains, of the weight of arrow points. Heavier points will remain at rest longer than lighter ones and will cause the arrow to bend more as the string pushes the nock end.

post sight: a type of bow sight with an aperture having a metal piece that projects up or down, the tip of which is lined up with the bull's-eye.

powder pouch: a container for talcum or similar powder used to dry the archer's hands.

pressure point: the spot on the arrow plate against which the arrow pushes upon release of the bowstring.

pull: to remove shot arrows from the target. Also, to draw the bow.

pushing: moving the bow forward and usually to the right during release.

quiver: a container for holding arrows. Most modern quivers attach to either the belt or the bow.

range: the place where archery shooting takes place. Also, the distance to be shot.

rebound: an arrow that hits the target face and bounces back toward the archer. Also called a *bounce out*.

recurve bow: a bow that curves forward at the limb tips.

reflexed bow: a bow that, although it may not have recurved limb tips, appears bent backward when unstrung.

release: to let go of the bowstring, ideally by relaxing the fingers and allowing the string to roll off them.

release aid: a mechanical device that hooks onto the bowstring to protect the archer's fingers. Today, about half of all archers use some kind of mechanical release aid.

ring sight: a bow sight with an aperture that is an open circle to be aligned with the bull's-eye.

Robin Hood: an accomplishment named after the legendary bowman, in which an archer shoots an arrow and drives its tip deep into the end of another arrow already in the target. Archers display their Robin Hoods as golfers display their hole-in-one balls.

round: a standardized unit of competition with a prescribed number of arrows to be shot at a prescribed distance or distances. There are rounds for all ability levels.

roving: an archery game in which a group of archers moves single file through the woods, shooting at random targets of unknown distances as designated by the first archer.

scatter: an arrow grouping in which the arrows are spread out over the target face or shooting area.

scoring area: the part of the target face made up of the scoring circles.

scratch score: an archer's score before it has been adjusted by a handicap.

self: a bow or arrow made from a single piece of wood.

serving: a protective wrapping of thread applied to the center portion of the bowstring to reduce wear.

shaft: the body of an arrow.

shelf: a horizontal projection at the bottom of the bow window upon which the arrow can lie if there is no arrow rest.

shooting glove: a protective leather covering that fits over the draw fingertips and attaches around the wrist, allowing a smooth release; an alternative to a finger tab.

shooting line: a marked line parallel to the targets from which all archers shoot.

sight: any device mounted on the bow that allows the archer to aim directly at the target.

sight bar: the part of the bow sight to which the aperture assembly is attached.

sight extension: a bar that allows the bow sight to be extended from the bow toward the target.

sight window: the recessed area just above the grip that allows the arrow to rest closer to the center of the bow.

six golds: a perfect end of six arrows.

skirt: the part of the target outside of the lowest scoring circle.

snake: said of an arrow that disappears in the grass.

snap shooting: a flaw in which the arrow is shot immediately as the bow sight aligns with the bull's-eye.

spent arrow: an arrow that has reached maximum velocity.

spine: the strength and flexibility of an arrow, measured by hanging a 2-pound weight from its center and noting its deflection. Spine must be matched with the draw weight of the bow.

spiral: the angle of the fletching relative to the arrow shaft.

square stance: shooting stance in which the line to the target runs from the toes of the back foot to the toes of the front foot to the target center.

stability: the ability of a bow, by merit of its design, to dampen small errors of form.

stabilizer: a small weight suspended a short distance from the front of the bow handle by a metal rod. A stabilizer adds weight to the bow and dampens torque and vibration.

stack: the rapid, disproportionate increase in limb resistance (draw weight) during the last few inches of draw.

stance: the foot position the archer assumes to address the target.

string: to attach the bowstring to the limb tips by bending the bow limbs, placing them under tension. Also, the bowstring itself.

string alignment: the relationship of the bowstring to the sight aperture.

string fingers: the fingers that draw back the bowstring (usually the three middle ones).

string height: see *brace height*.

string notch: the grooves near each limb tip into which the loops of the bowstring fit when the bow is braced.

style: the type of shooting equipment used by the archer, such as freestyle, freestyle limited, barebow, competitive bowhunter, bowhunter freestyle, and bowhunter freestyle limited.

tackle: archery equipment in general, including bows, arrows, strings, quivers, armguards, and gloves.

takedown bow: a bow with detachable limbs.

target archery: the sport of shooting arrows accurately over long distances ranging from 30 to 90 meters (33 to 99 yards). A set number of arrows are usually shot at several distances to complete a tournament round.

target arrow: a lightweight arrow with a target point.

target captain: the person at each target during a tournament whose job it is to call the scoring value of all arrows at that target.

target face: the paper or cardboard scoring area mounted on the target butt.

target panic: the inability to hold the sight steady on the bull's-eye.

tassel: a woolen cloth that hangs from the archer's belt or quiver, used to wipe dirt from the shafts of arrows. Some clubs adopt a specific color for use by their members.

tiller: a measure of even balance in the two limbs. The tiller on a compound bow is changed by adjusting the limb bolts, which varies the distance between the base of the limb and the string.

timber: warning call to other archers who may be in the danger zone, alerting them that an arrow has been released or is about to be released.

tip: the end of an arrow point or bow limb.

torque: twisting the bow along its long axis at release.

toxology: the study of archery.

toxophilite: an archer or a lover of archery.

traditional draw length: Distance at full draw from the back of the bow—the side away from the archer—to the nock end of the arrow.

trajectory: the parabolic path of an arrow in flight.

tuning: adjustment of the arrow spine, arrow rest, pressure point, cushion plunger, string height, tiller, and nocking point to perfect arrow flight.

underbowed: said of an archer using a bow too light in draw weight.

understrung: a bow with too long a string, resulting in a brace height too low for efficient shooting.

vane: plastic arrow fletching, more wind- and waterproof than feathers but usually heavier.

wand: a narrow stick or piece of tape used as a target.

wand shooting: an event or game in which archers shoot at a piece of tape set vertically on a target face.

weight: the number of pounds of force required to draw the bowstring a given distance.

windage: compensating to the left or the right to allow for drift due to wind.

wrist sling: a strap that wraps around the archer's wrist and the bow handle to prevent the bow from falling to the ground upon release.

yaw: erratic motion of an arrow on its flight to the target. Also called *wobble*.

RESOURCES

....

NATIONAL ARCHERY ASSOCIATION

The National Archery Association of the United States (NAA) is recognized by archery's international body, FITA, and the United States Olympic Committee as the organization responsible for selecting and training the men's and women's Olympic archery teams. The NAA is responsible for presenting teams at the world championships and Pan-Am Games. The NAA also conducts annual national championships, which determine champions in a variety of age groups and shooting styles.

Even if you're not a potential champion, the NAA has something to offer. If you're interested in shooting at targets with a recurve bow, this is the organization to join. If you prefer to shoot a compound bow, the NAA has a growing division for compounds with release aids.

Benefits of membership in the NAA include the following:
- Membership in your NAA state association
- NAA membership card and decal
- Subscription to NAA publications
- Competition and instruction in club programs
- Instructor and coach certification
- Leadership opportunities on local, state, and national committees and boards
- Annual state and national rankings
- Liability insurance
- Discounts on NAA and USAT items
- Training camps
- Event notices and updates
- "Sport for a lifetime" friendships
- Opportunity to become a member of the U.S. Archery Teams

The NAA has many state and local affiliates. These clubs and associations provide year-round competition and training for target archery, indoors and out. This is where most target archers get started and where most continue their practice.

Below are listed the adult archery clubs affiliated with the NAA. There are actually more clubs for juniors than for adults under the NAA umbrella, but space does not allow for their inclusion here. Contact the NAA or one of the groups below to find the junior club nearest you.

For more information, contact the National Archery Association, One Olympic Plaza, Colorado Springs, CO 80909, telephone (719) 578-4576, fax (719) 632-4733.

Adult Archery Clubs

Ace Archers, Manning Baumgardner, 4849 Herndon Dr., Dublin, OH 43221

All American Hunting and Survival Club, A. Jauregui, 19015 Parthenia St., #E, Northridge, CA 91324

Angel Sports Club, 7-12 Higashiueno 1-Chome, Taito-Ku, Tokyo 110, Japan 00012

Archery and Computer Sales, Conrad Kennedy, Rt. 8, Box 457, Hwy. at I-10, Beaumont, TX 77705

Aripeka Archers Club, Tim Wanat, 7522 Clanton Trail, Hudson, FL 34667-3063

Arizona State Archers Association, Terry LaBeau, 3500 W. Peterson Place, Tucson, AZ 85741

Auroraland Archers, Joe Casado, 1293 Herrington Rd., Geneva, IL 60134

Bedford Park Archery Club, Stan Goldys, 6700 S. 78th Ave., Bedford Park, IL 60501

Big Apple Archery Lanes, Al Lizzio, 170-20 39th Ave., Flushing, NY 11358-2261

Bloomfield Archers, Maureen Tarantino, 13-09 20th St., Fair Lawn, NJ 07410

British Long-Bow Society, Al Partridge, 82 Brimwood Dr., Vernon, CT 06066

Brown County Archery Association, Dana Florestand, P.O. Box

30089, Indianapolis, IN 46230

Cape May County Archery Association, Scott McGonigle, P.O. Box 261, Cape May Court House, NJ 08210

Chemung City Rod and Gun Club, Bob Stansfield, 308 Watkins Rd., Horseheads, NY 14845

Chieftain Archery Club, Violette Shank, 2732 Lehigh St., Lower Burrell, PA 15068

Cincinnati Archery Club, Teresa Brothers, 6158 Price Rd., Loveland, OH 45140-9127

Cleveland Archery Club, Tina Less, 16431 Cypress Ave., Strongsville, OH 44136

Columbus FITA Archers, Jim Shull, 379 Stanbery Ave., Columbus, OH 43209

Connecticut Target Archers Association, Tricia Johnson, 291 W. Middle Turnpike, Manchester, CT 06040

Crescent Bowmen Archery, Nick Graham, 10116 Leacrest Rd., Cincinnati, OH 45215

Denton County Archers, Carl Dane, P.O. Box 328, Aubrey, TX 76227

Dupage Target Archers, Don Branson, P.O. Box 684, Wheaton, IL 60189

Eastern Archery Association, Dave McCullough, 7210 McCullough Rd., Sharpsville, PA 16150

Fairfax Target Archers, Leroy Anderson, 9202 Cutting Horse Ct., Springfield, VA 22153

FITA Archers of Ohio Association, Larry Michael, 4890 Lithopolis Winchester, Canal Winchester, OH 43110

FITA Archers of Pennsylvania, Eugene Prokop, P.O. Box 95, Hatboro, PA 19040

Flood City Bowmen, Henry Rummel, 725 Bloom St., Johnstown, PA 15902-1810

Florida Archery Association, Timothy Austin, 3029 NW 38th St., Gainesville, FL 32606-8119

Florida FITA Club, Edward Newbern, P.O. Box 4171, Deland, FL 32723

Fort Lauderdale Archers, Judy Glaser, 6614 Pebble Beach, N. Lauderdale, FL 33068

Golden Gate Archers, Jon Ray, 5180 Oxbow Ct., San Jose, CA 95124

Golden North Archery Club, Rick Schikora, Box 70254, Fairbanks, AK 99707

Gold-N-Grain Archery, Deann McCullough, 75 McCullough Rd., Sharpsville, PA 16150

Hawaii State Archers Association, Lawrence Paglinawan, 2924 Kaimuki Ave., Honolulu, HI 96816

Hemlock Field Archery, Ed Overdier, P.O. Box 222, Cornwall, PA 17016-0222

Illinois Target Archery Association, Ben Pitchkites, 513 N. Emerson, Mt. Prospect, IL 60056

Indiana Archery Association, Dana Florestand, P.O. Box 30089, Indianapolis, IN 46230-0089

Jardin de l'Arc Brisé, Craig Clifford, 600 West Long, Stephenville, TX 76401

Kansas FITA & Saint Archery Association, Jim Mellinger, 1929 S. Spruce, Wichita, KS 67211

Lee County Bowhunters, Tim Walker, 1316 Driftwood Dr., N. Fort Myers, FL 33903

Liberty Archers, James Casey, 951 Highway 90 W., Defuniak Springs, FL 32433

Massachusetts Hospital School, Dick Crisafulli, 3 Randolph St., Canton, MA 02021

Massachusetts State Archery Association, Verna Semple, P.O. Box 3322, Wareham, MA 02571-3322

Michigan Amateur Club, Earl Meyers, 329 West Pine, Fremont, MI 49412-1533

Nassau Bowmen, William Argyropoulos, 26 Lincoln Blvd., Hempstead, NY 11550-1433

The National Crossbowmen, Rolfe Smith, 398 E. Street Rd., Kennett Square, PA 19348

National Field Archery Association, Paul Double, 8129 Bennett Branch Rd., Mt. Airy, MD 21771

N.E.S.A. Archers, Marcia Wyman, 109 School St., Concord, NH 03301

New Jersey Archery Association, Eileen Pylypchuk, 355 W. Passaic Ave., Bloomfield, NJ 07003-5521

Norfolk Archery Club, Box 505, Norfolk, NE 68702-0505

Northern Archery Association, Doug Brothers, 6158 Price Rd., Loveland, OH 45140

Order of Saint Sebastian Archers, Deane Geiken, 309 E. Pells, Paxton, IL 60957

Oriole Archers, Jack Treadwell, 25 Thomas Shilling Ct., Upperco, MD 21155

Pacific Bowmen NAA, Lawrence Paglinawan, 1344 Young St., #6, Honolulu, HI 96814

Paradise Archers, Bob Graham, 67-392 Mission Dr., Cathedral City, CA 92234-5012

Penn State Archery Association, Barbara Goss, RD 1 Box 247A, Lewistown, PA 17044

Rakowana Archery Club, L. Michael Leonard, East Shore Dr., East Berne, NY 12059

Reading Archery Club, Karen Wolf, P.O. Box 122, Shillington, PA 19607-0122

Rhode Island Archery Association, James Dean, 140 Poplar Dr., Cranston, RI 02920

Sacramento Archery Club, Robyn Horn, 2313 22nd Ave., Sacramento, CA 95822

Sandeas Archery Club, Lloyd Brown-Arco TC, 1750 Wueste Rd., Chula Vista, CA 91915

San Joaquin Valley Target Archers, P.O. Box 596, Edison, CA 93220-0596

Seattle Archery Federation, Joe St. Charles, 19807 1st Ave. S., Seattle, WA 98148

Society for Archery in Michigan, Glenn Meyers, 329 W. Pine, Fremont, MI 49412

State Archers of California, Tom Green, 9830 Tavernor Rd., Wilton, CA 95693

State of Maine Archery Center, Richard Bryant, 3 Lori Dr., Brunswick, ME 04011-1620

Summit Archers, Robert Wolcheck, 31 Edgewood Rd., Chatham, NJ 07928-1518

Target Archers of Maryland, William Light, 1107 Greenway Rd., Cockeysville, MD 21030-1707

Target Archers of North Carolina, Ruby Wooten, 2233 Marble St., Winston-Salem, NC 27107-3510

Texas State Archery Association, Irene Jenkins, P.O. Box 140171, Austin, TX 78714

Three Rivers Archery Club, Cathy Korby, 7979 Countryside Lane, Willow River, MN 55795

Tucson Target Archers, Ed Manley, P.O. Box 43925, Tucson, AZ 85733-3925

Two Flags, Inc., Bob Exley, HC-34, Box 345, New Castle, VA 24127

Utah FITA Archers, Randi Smith, 348 E. Stonehedge #15B, Salt Lake City, UT 84107-1846

Utah Wheelchair/Amateur Archers, Larry Smith, 1130 E. Wilmington Ave., Salt Lake City, UT 84106

Valkyrie Archery Club, Betty Bakken, 807 E. Main, Mt. Horeb, WI 53572

Virginia Archery Association, Deborah Ryder, 1210 Edgewood Dr., Harrisonburg, VA 22801-3502

Washington State Archery Association, Jody Dickey, 6914 SE Dorlane Ct., Port Orchard, WA 98366-9022

Western Oregon FITA Archery, Alan Gerard, 82581 Barbre Rd., Dexter, OR 97431

Wood Bow Club of Utah, Dan Perry, 184 East 705 South, Salem, UT 84653

Wo-Pe-Na Archers, Maureen Tarantino, 13-09 20th St., Fair Lawn, NJ 07410

Wyoming State Archery Association, Larry Baker, 437 Warren, Thermopolis, WY 82443

NATIONAL FIELD ARCHERY ASSOCIATION

The National Field Archery Association is the governing body for field archery in the United States. At the grassroots of field archery are local archery clubs that participate in this kind of shooting. They are located all over the United States. Most local clubs are affiliated with a state association that organizes championships and regional tournaments. Becoming a member is easy and inexpensive. Ask at any archery shop or sporting-goods store.

For more information, contact the NFAA at 31407 Outer I-10, Redlands, CA 92373, telephone (909) 794-2133.